THE BOOK OF THE SHARK

THE BOOK OF THE SHARK

DR KEITH BANNISTER

THE APPLE PRESS

A QUINTET BOOK

Published by The Apple Press
6 Blundell Street
London, N7 9BH

ISBN 1-85076-123-X

This book was designed and produced by
Quintet Publishing Limited
6 Blundell Street
London N7 9BH

Creative Director: Peter Bridgewater
Designer: Jonathan Roberts
Project Editor: Shaun Barrington
Editor: Mike Darton

Typeset in Great Britain by
Central Southern Typesetters, Eastbourne
Manufactured in Hong Kong by
Regent Publishing Services Limited
Printed in Hong Kong by
Leefung-Asco Printers Limited

PICTURE CREDITS AND ACKNOWLEDGEMENTS

Captain Ned Middleton pp 6, 88; Jack Jackson,
back cover, pp 8, 87a, 111; Rolf Willams pp 9
(middle), 17, 25b, 27, 32, 34, 51, 52, 55, 61, 90, 109;
Al Ristori pp 10, 12, 40, 56, 60, 79, 93a, 98; Dr Guido
Dingerkus pp 15b, 25a, 31, 64, 73, 99, 115a, 121,
122, 124; Ardea London – Ron and Valerie Taylor,
front cover, pp 15a, 20, 44, 47, 48, 49, 50, 67, 68,
69, 70, 76, 82, 85, 91b, 106 – P Morris pp 29, 81;
Alex Double pp 18, 26, 62; A.G.E. Fotostock, Barce-
lona, pp 22, 36, 112; Dr Keith Bannister pp 33, 38;
Michael Freeman p 54; Hulton Picture Library pp 57,
58, 59 (inset), 74; Ramon Munoz-Chapuli pp 59, 65,
72, 84, 86, 102, 103, 114, 115b, 117b, 120; Oxford
Scientific Films – Rudie H Kuiter pp 66, 93b, 125 –
Godfrey Merlen p 87b – Miriam Austerman p 96; Sea
World, Florida, pp 91a, 92; Doug Perrine p 94; Robert
Irving p 105; G H Burgess pp 118, 119.

The author and publishers would like to thank Robert
Irving, G H Burgess and Senor Ramon Munoz-Chapuli
for their contributions of information and images to
this book.

Illustrations are by Pat Shaw, Robert Irving and Rolf
Williams.

CONTENTS

CHAPTER ONE

ANATOMY OF A SHARK

The Bull shark, *Carcharhinus leucas;* the most feared of the family *Carcharhinidae,* along with the Tiger shark. It is quite easy to classify a shark according to order — and even, usually, family — by its external anatomy. Correctly identifying genus and species is quite a different matter: no one knows, for example, just how many shark attacks are by the Bull shark, because it is not readily differentiated. All sharks of the order Carchariniformes — more than 200 species — have one anal fin, two spineless dorsal fins, five gill slits and a nictitating membrane over the eye.

The general shape of a shark is well known. The streamlined body, the pointed snout overhanging the curved mouth lined with sharp teeth, the sinister triangle of the dorsal fin – all are commonly portrayed features of these elegant animals. Such features are, however, only part of the story; in this chapter a more complete account is given.

First, there is no such thing as a typical or standard shark. For example, in relation simply to the fins, some species have one dorsal fin, others have two. The anal fin is important (see page 62). Five orders have one anal fin, three have none, so the distinction is a first step in building up the picture of order, family, genus and species. Qualifying adjectives such as 'most' or 'some' are therefore often used to indicate that there is a great deal of variation within this circumscribed group of animals.

EXTERNAL FEATURES

The body shape varies widely. Not all sharks are streamlined for leisurely swimming and fast hunting, although that body shape is common to many and frequently seen in illustrations of sharks that are fished by rod and line – the Mako shark (*Isurus* spp.), the Tiger shark (*Galeocerdo cuvieri*), the Blue shark (*Prionace glauca*) and many species of the genus *Carcharhinus* (the White-tip shark, Bull shark, Silky shark, Lemon shark, etc.). Such a shape, although relatively common, contrasts markedly with the eel-like shape of the Frilled shark (*Chlamydoselachus anguineus*);

Below right ■ Grey reef shark *Carcharhinus amblyrhynchos*, photographed at a reef drop-off in the Red Sea. Sharks of the genus *Carcharhinus* exemplify the 'classic' streamlined shape of many fast hunting sharks.

indeed, the species name *anguineus* is actually the Latin word for 'snake'. Many of the Cat sharks (eg *Haploblepharus* and *Schroederichthys* spp.) have body shapes somewhere between the idealized shape and that of the Frilled shark. The Port Jackson sharks (*Heterodontus* spp.) have a very stocky body with an almost bovine head. The Humantin (*Oxynotus* sp.) has a deep body, nearly triangular in cross section, and a ridged back supporting very tall dorsal fins. Angel sharks (*Squatina* spp.) are flattened and look very like rays. The Saw sharks (*Pristiophorus* sp. and *Pliotrema warreni*) are also flattened, but slender, and have a very long rostrum that gives them their common name (see *Pristiophoriformes* Species List p123).

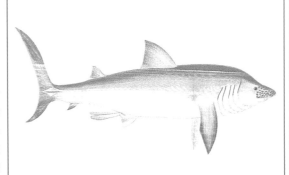

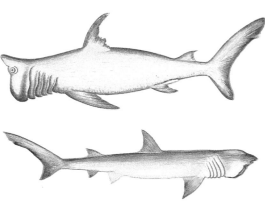

Left ■ A baby Lemon shark — less than a year old — just before release. Scientific study of sharks has, thankfully, begun to wear away common misconceptions and fears about these supremely adapted creatures.

Inaccurate and exaggerated illustrations of early natural history books are well known, and these examples are no exception. Without the aid of photographs, the artist had to rely on the occasional dead specimen and, if none was available, a lot of imagination. The Basking shark (*top left*), for example, possesses a head bearing more than a passing resemblance to a seal. At least certain basic characteristics were correct, including (*bottom left*) five gill slits and an asymmetrical tail fin.

Opposite ■ After a struggle that may last for several hours, a 'defeated' Mako shark is held aloft. The teeth and jaws of such specimens may be kept as souvenirs by game fishermen.

Right, Top to Bottom ■ *Dagger-nose shark Isogomphodon oxyrhynchus;* Thresher shark *Alopias vulpinus;* Graceful shark *Carcharhinus amblyrhynchoides;* Portuguese shark *Centroscymnus coelolepis.* The classification of sharks depends upon numerous factors, including the number of fins and gill slits, the position of the mouth and shape of the snout.

In almost all sharks, the body tapers in front of the tail to form the caudal peduncle. Fast-swimming open-ocean sharks may have one or two lateral keels on the peduncle which help to reduce water resistance so that much of the shark's muscular power is transferred into the tail fin, which then produces its main thrust in swimming.

Examples of different body shapes are shown below. Most sharks have triangular dorsal fins. There are commonly two, the first most often larger than the second, but in some species only one (the posterior, above the anal fin) is present. The leading edge of the dorsal fins may be strengthened with a spine. In the smallest of all sharks, *Squaliolus laticauda,* the first dorsal fin is little more than just a spine.

The pectoral fins are broad-based, and located just behind – and in some cases, partly below – the gill slits. As with all the fins in sharks, but unlike the fins of bony fishes, the pectoral fins cannot be folded back, and are consequently erect all the time. To a shark, these fins function much as the wings do on an aircraft: cross-sections of the shape of the pectoral fins prove that the design and the effect of both are remarkably similar. With a forward motion, the pressure is increased below and decreased above, thereby lifting the shark without the expenditure of extra energy or the development of special organs with a hydrostatic function.

The paired pelvic fins are located at about the midpoint of the underside of the shark's body. In males, each fin is modified into a penis-like intro-

Right ■ The enlarged upper caudal lobe distinguishes the Thresher shark from all others. Because of this feature, this shark was also known in times past as the Fox shark.

mittent structure called a clasper. The reason behind the name is possibly that the fins are armed with hook-like denticles thought to hold on to the female while sperm is transferred. The clasper is erectile and has a complex skeleton; its function is described in more detail later.

Anal fins may be absent, or there may be one which varies in size according to species. Its function is identical to that of dorsal fins: to prevent rolling. The absence or presence of the anal fin is important in shark classification.

The tail fin (the caudal fin) has a basic hetero-cercal shape – that is, its upper lobe is bigger than its lower lobe. In sharks, but only very rarely in bony fish, the vertebral column runs into the upper lobe of the tail fin, with the result that the tail fin's lobes are asymmetrical both internally and externally. The lower lobe, not supported by the cartilaginous vertebral column, is instead stiffened by a series of flexible cartilaginous elements (radials) articulating with the underside of the spine.

The shape of its tail is of great importance to the swimming of a shark: an examination of the shape reveals the shark's lifestyle. Sharks with the most symmetrical (lunate) tails are, like bony fishes with tails of a similar shape, fast swimmers. Such a lunate tail most commonly projects from a narrow caudal peduncle with a small pit in the back just in front of the upper lobe. The function of the pit is unknown. Sharks with this type of caudal fin usually have lateral keels on the peduncle to increase swimming efficiency.

Some sharks – such as the Thresher shark (*Alopias vulpinus*) –have a greatly enlarged upper caudal lobe. This is a specialization used in catching prey. Slug-gish sharks have a greatly reduced caudal fin, and swim with a clumsy eel-like motion. Examples of different types of caudal fins are illustrated on page 14.

Sharks do not have scales, as do bony fish. Instead, the skin is invested with large numbers of usually very small thorn-like structures or denticles. They consist of a basal plate embedded in the dermis, and a distal sharp process (the 'thorn' or hook) pointing backwards. This arrangement means that if a shark is rubbed from head to tail – ie in the direction of the denticles' thorns – the skin is relatively

smooth, but if it is rubbed in the other direction the skin has a rasp-like character. The shape of the denticles varies between species, and can be an invaluable aid in species identification. Most denticles are too small to be observed in detail without a microscope. In some sharks, however – eg the aptly named Bramble shark (*Echinorhinus* spp.) – there are very few, but very large, denticles.

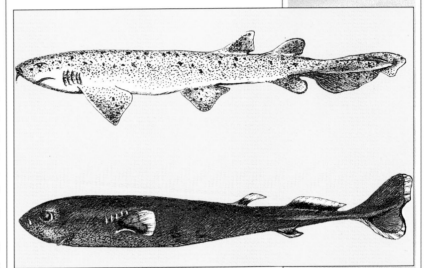

The Nursehound, *Scylorhinus stellaris*, (above) is classified in a completely different order to *Euprotomicrus bispinatus* (below) for several reasons, the most obvious to a non-specialist being the variation in fin arrangement.

THE SKELETON

The skeleton is made of cartilage, a flexible, tough gristle-like material, present as the precursor of bone in other vertebrates. Some parts of the skeleton of sharks may be calcified to strengthen it where it is subject to mechanical stress.

The shark's skull (the cranium) is a single, compact, cartilaginous block enclosing the brain and the olfactory and auditory capsules; through it run the foramina (small corridors) for the passage of nerves and bloodvessels. Lateral cavities protect the eyes. In some species the skull is extended anteriorly, forming a rostrum – this is most marked in the Saw sharks. The jaws are attached loosely to the under-surface of the cranium and to a separate short rod of cartilage in front of, and formerly in series with, the gill arches. Details of the attachment of the jaws to the cranium are of great importance in elucidating aspects of shark evolution.

The gill arches are formed of cartilaginous rods that hoop around the contours of the body. Most sharks have five gill slits, but a few species have six, and some seven.

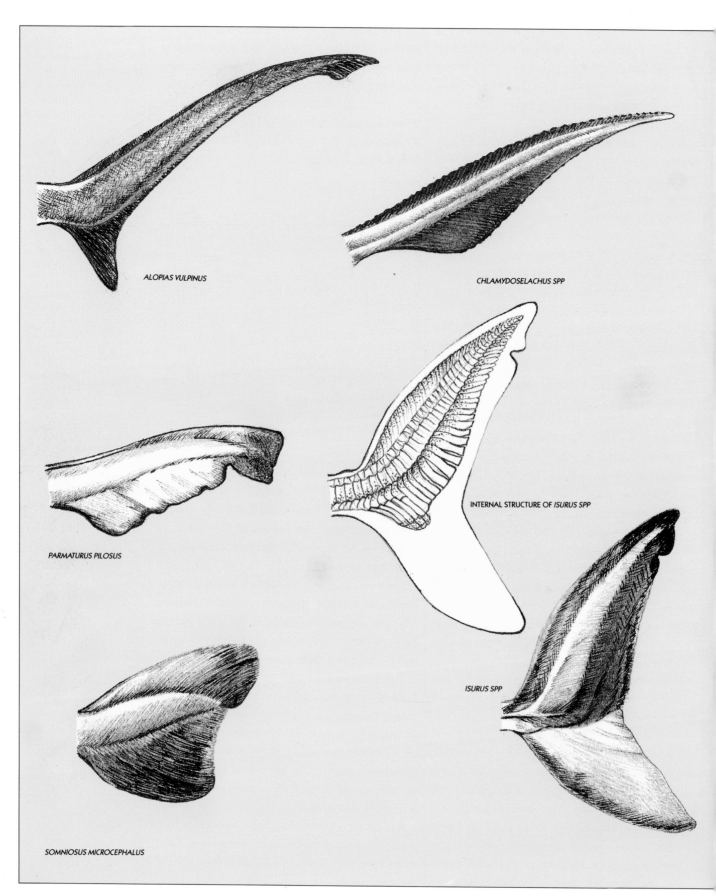

ALOPIAS VULPINUS

CHLAMYDOSELACHUS SPP

PARMATURUS PILOSUS

INTERNAL STRUCTURE OF ISURUS SPP

ISURUS SPP

SOMNIOSUS MICROCEPHALUS

Examples of different types of caudal fin; sharks with extended upper caudal lobes (*top left*) may use them to help swing the body from side to side during swimming (as does the Tiger shark), or for stunning prey (as the Thresher shark is thought to do). Those which are more symmetrical in shape have been evolved by certain species (for example the Great White and the Porbeagle) for both low-speed cruising and high-speed dashes after fast-moving prey.

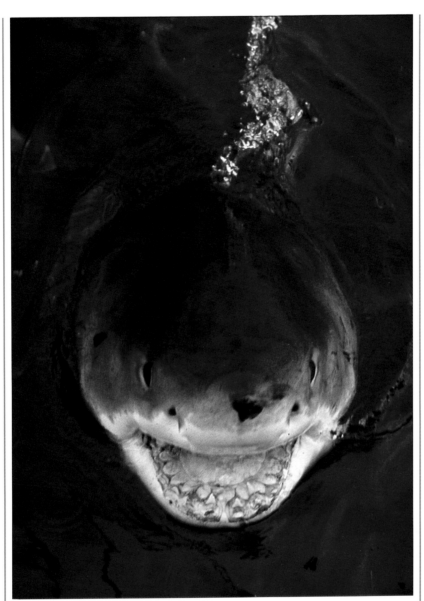

Left ■ As with most other sharks, the teeth of the Great White are continually being moved to the front of the jaw, where eventually they will work loose, often becoming embedded in their victim's flesh.

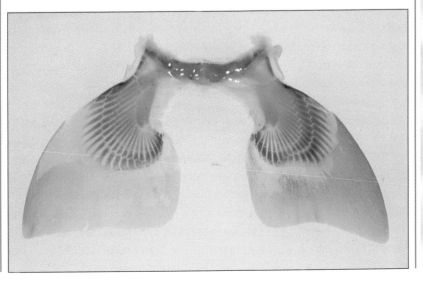

Left ■ The pectoral girdle of the Smooth Dogfish *Mustelus canis*. The skeletal elements of all sharks are primarily composed of cartilage, one of the main characteristics that distinguishes them from the bony fish.

The vertebral column is flexible, as is readily deduced by anyone who sees a shark swim. Each segment of the vertebral column – each vertebra – consists of an articulating portion (the centrum) surmounted by an arch that protects the spinal cord. Although there is no ribcage as such in sharks, small non-supportive processes from part of each centrum are believed to represent reduced ribs. The vertebral column extends almost to the very end of the upper lobe of the caudal fin. The other fins are supported by simple cartilaginous rods with various configurations. The pectoral fin skeleton is secured to the vertebral column by a stout pectoral girdle. The pelvic girdle is not supported and lies in the ventral muscle layers. The most complex fin skeleton is that of the claspers.

THE TEETH

If sharks have one attribute more famous than any other it is their teeth.

The mouth is well provided with teeth that have an enamelled blade with one or more points (or cusps). A common shape is that shown by the teeth of Sand sharks: a large, pointed central cusp and two small lateral cusps. The shape varies between species. In some species tooth shape is different in each jaw and may also vary according to the position of the tooth in the jaw. The hard enamel covering provides the sharp cutting edge for which the shark's teeth are famed.

The size of the teeth varies widely. Tooth size is not directly related to overall body size, however. Those of the two largest sharks, for example – the Basking shark and the Whale shark – are minute, forming bands that are little more than file-like. Unlike the teeth of many vertebrates, including our own, that wear down and are lost with age, sharks' teeth are naturally replaced throughout life, gradually moving to the front of the jaw. Worn or loose teeth drop out at the front of the jaw, each to be replaced by the one behind it. The teeth form behind the cartilage of the jaw. There is a whole whorl of replacement teeth constantly increasing in size, lying flat at first, but springing up as they move over the rim of the jaw. In most sharks the teeth are used for seizing or cutting; in only a few sharks (the Port Jackson sharks) are the teeth developed for grinding.

A few deep-sea sharks have been found when caught to have some of their own teeth in their stomachs, and it is thought that they may consciously swallow them to re-utilize the minerals in the teeth, for such minerals are a scarcity in the deep sea. Because of the enamel, shark teeth are well preserved and common as fossils. Indeed, many fossil sharks are known only by their teeth.

The large filter-feeding sharks do not use their teeth to feed. Instead, plankton is filtered from the water as it flows out through the gill slits by a network of enlarged gill rakers (see Basking shark, later).

In several sharks (eg *Apristurus riveri*) the teeth of the male are much larger than those of the female. This, and the much thicker skin around the neck and back of the female, provide evidence that the male bites the female to hold on to her during mating – behaviour witnessed in the Grey Reef shark.

THE ALIMENTARY CANAL

The alimentary canal – the gut – in sharks is a long tube running from the mouth to the rectum and anus. The stomach is a large U-shaped expansion, from which runs the short intestine. Food is digested in the stomach and its nutrients are absorbed in the intestine. The stomach in some sharks is elastic to accommodate large prey or, in the case of the Swell sharks, to take up quantities of water to inflate the shark in order to deter a predator.

A vital factor in acquiring nourishment is the surface area of the intestine through which relevant elements of the digested food can be absorbed. Sharks have a short intestine which, were it just a simple tube, would be an inefficient absorber. For efficiency, therefore, the surface area is greatly increased by means of a 'spiral valve'. In its simplest form this consists of an absorptive membrane that runs like a spiral staircase along the length of the intestine. Its form and degree of elaboration varies between species. This feature is found in all sharks but in very few other fishes.

In the rectum is a small sausage-shaped gland, the rectal gland. Although conspicuous, its function is uncertain. It has been suggested, however, that the gland may be involved in secreting excess salt in the body fluids as part of the osmoregulatory system of the shark.

The liver forms two large lobes that occupy a large proportion of the abdominal cavity. Here much of the digested nutriment is stored as oil, and it is for this oil that many sharks have been hunted. Sharks have no swimbladder to aid buoyancy as do bony fish, and it has long been suggested that this absence has been compensated for by the oil in the liver (oil being lighter than water). Recent critical studies have nevertheless suggested that the contribution of this oil reservoir to buoyancy may not be as substantial as had been surmised.

long artery running to the tail along the underside of the spinal column. From this dorsal artery, other arteries branch off to supply the liver, stomach, kidneys, and other organs and muscles.

The used blood, its oxygen having been absorbed by the cells, is collected by small capillaries. These merge into progressively larger vessels and into large blood-filled spaces called sinuses, by means of which the blood is returned to the heart. The venous return is comparatively sluggish, for the veins do not have elastic walls to maintain pressure as ours do.

Below Left ■ The gut contents of sharks may reveal the remains of recent prey species. However, surprises are not uncommon: this False Catshark *Pseudotriakis microdon* was found to have some potatoes, a pear, orange peel, a plastic bag, a Coca-cola can and a cigar wrapper in its stomach.

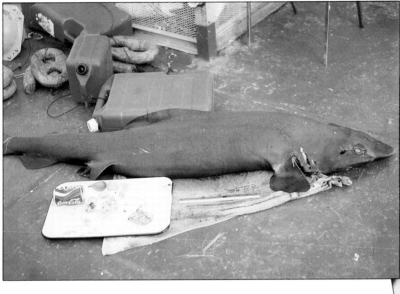

THE BLOOD CIRCULATION

Like us, sharks have a heart to pump oxygenated blood through the arteries. They also have veins to return the oxygen-depleted blood to the heart. Their veins, though, are less well formed than ours and more often resemble tunnels between muscle blocks.

The heart lies protected in a cartilaginous chamber near the ventral surface between the pectoral fins. The single ventricle pumps the blood along the ventral aorta, lying between the bottoms of the gill slits. The ventral aorta divides to send a branch up to each gill bar where it progressively further divides into minute bloodvessels with very thin walls. Through these walls a gas exchange takes place: the blood becomes oxygenated by its close proximity to the oxygen in the seawater, losing carbon dioxide into the sea simultaneously. The now oxygenated blood is gathered up at the top of the gills into a single

The vessels from all over the body meet at the sinus venosus – a 'bag' on top of the ventricle. From there blood goes into the atrium, then the ventricle, and the pumping cycle pushes it forward to the gills for re-oxygenation.

Red blood cells are formed in the spleen or in the bloodvessels themselves. The red colour stems from the presence of the pigmented protein haemoglobin, which acts as the oxygen-carrying agent within the blood (as it does in humans too). White blood corpuscles are formed mostly in the gonads.

The kidneys remove much of the waste products from the blood. Shark kidneys are long blood-rich organs, consisting of elongated convoluted tubules forming a long flat patch each side of the ventral surface of the vertebral column. In an eviscerated shark they can be seen as two long, dark red stripes in that position.

Above ■ Essentially, a shark has no throat, as this view of a bonnethead shows; the gill slits are clearly visible. Whatever will fit in the shark's mouth goes straight into the stomach.

CHAPTER TWO

SHARK SENSES

With its eyes widely set on its
intriguingly shaped head, a
Hammerhead shark quietly
patrols the ocean's blue surface
waters.

The head of a Blue shark *Prionace glauca* clearly displays the nasal opening covered by a flap of skin. A current of water is directed into the nostril, allowing very low concentrations of chemicals to be detected by the sensory lamellae in the nasal sacs.

Sharks, like all vertebrates, have brains. A brain is an enlarged and complex mass of neural tissue that receives information from the environment, interprets and orders this information, and causes an appropriate response from the body. The shark brain's structure, however, is much simpler than a mammalian brain and has accordingly been studied in order by comparison to elucidate the structural complexities of our own brains: it is still studied by biology students as an example of an archetypal vertebrate brain.

The vertebrate brain is divided into three parts, each part having its own specific functions. In the shark these parts can easily be seen. They are present in the the human brain but relative differential growth has obscured their original simple linear arrangement. The three segments are called the fore-brain, mid-brain and hind-brain.

Although there is much loose jocular reference to brain size, the significance of brain size to its possessor is not clear. The common presumption is that mammals, being more advanced (ie culminat-

Sharks can learn. They can be trained, on a simple reward basis, to distinguish between different shapes. The results of learning experiments will ultimately provide us with an idea of what a shark can perceive. It is, for example, easier for a shark to distinguish between a square and a diamond than a square and a circle. In another experiment Lemon sharks have been trained to respond differently to white and red. The latter trial did not reveal if the sharks were seeing white and red, or whether they were seeing different degrees of brightness. More elaborate experiments using more advanced physiological-technological techniques have since been used to provide that answer.

Some authorities contend that sharks play. Playing is regarded as a learning process or an occupation forming a relaxation for an intellectually well developed animal. In either case, in the context of sharks, such attributions must be treated with a great deal of caution: a shark's interaction with objects in a situation that does not seem to have any obvious purpose should not be described as 'playing' for want of any other word to describe such behaviour.

Sharks are sentient animals. They have the same five senses that we have – smell, sight, sound, taste and touch. In addition they can receive other forms of information from the environment which we cannot. They can detect electromagnetic waves outside human range and they also have a sense of so-called 'distant touch'.

SMELL

A flap on the outside of a shark's nostrils effectively separates the nasal opening into an inner and an outer aperture and directs the water current into the outer opening. Inside the nasal capsule the water flows over an elaborate array of sensory lamellae where odours are detected. The sampled water then leaves through the upper aperture. The olfactory lamellae are close to the olfactory lobe, an outgrowth of the fore-brain.

Both the physical closeness of the sensory part of the nasal cavity to the brain and the results of experimental research suggest that smell is a very important sense to sharks.

Some classic experiments were conducted in the early years of this century on the sense of smell in

ing in humans), have relatively the largest brains among the vertebrates. However, if the major vertebrate groups are rated by the ratio of brain weight to body weight this ratio is discovered to be higher in sharks than in most bony fishes and in many birds, and about equal to the lower third of the mammal range. What this ratio measures in terms of, say, intellect is uncertain. But it does show that sharks do not have small brains. And among the sharks, the carcharinids have bigger brains and the squalids have smaller.

The Starry Smoothhound *Mustelus asterias* is a member of the houndshark family. It is found in coastal waters close to the seabed, where it feeds on invertebrates, particularly crustaceans. The white spots on its dorsal surface distinguish it from other smoothhounds, and though these may align close to the lateral line, they are not thought to perform any sensory function.

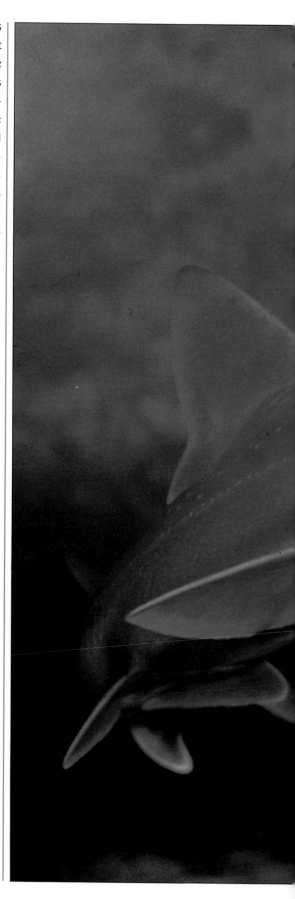

the Smoothhound *Mustelus canis*. This species is often the subject of experimental work because it thrives in captivity. The technique was to tempt the fish with the body fluids from freshly killed crabs (crabs form an important part of their diet). In captivity the dogfish were habituated to taking first live crabs, then freshly killed and punctured crabs, and next disguised dead crabs. Once the Smoothhounds could detect disguised crabs, other inorganic objects similarly disguised were offered to the dogfish – but any such inorganic items were ignored and the disguised crab was always chosen. To test that it was indeed smell that they were using, the dogfish's nostrils were plugged. The crabs then could not be distinguished from the other offerings. In an extension of the initial experiment, only one nostril was plugged. In this case the dogfish, as might have been expected, in the presence of a scent always turned in the direction of the open nostril. If that action took the fish outside the scent range, it turned back until the food was located. In a while the dogfish learned to some extent to compensate for its reduced directional sense of smell.

Much later it was discovered that the sense of smell is greatly enhanced in starving sharks. Under the right conditions, and with a sufficiently attractive essence, sharks can smell a substance in a dilution of 1 in 10^9.

HEARING AND 'DISTANT TOUCH'

Sharks may seem not to have any ears, but they do have. Our ears – the external parts we see – do not have any genuinely auditory function: they are mammalian devices that collect and channel the soundwaves, and help to locate a sound source. In some other mammals ears may have an important ornamental function. The actual 'hearing' is done in the inner ear. Perhaps confusingly, the original function of the auditory organ was not for hearing at all, but was for balance, for establishing the equilibrium of the body. It is probable that the earliest vertebrates did not hear at all. The considerable auditory ability of, particularly, mammals stems from a specialized outgrowth – the cochlea – from the floor of the internal ear of lower vertebrates. The balancing equipment remains and is fully functional in our own ears. Its structure is still much like that in sharks.

The semicircular canals of the shark's inner ear. The three canals are fluid-filled and are arranged to lie at right angles to each other, thereby allowing movement to be detected in any plane.

The primitive vertebrate ear, exemplified by the anatomy of sharks, consists of three semicircular canals, two in opposed vertical planes and one in a horizontal plane. The three canals are confluent ventrally with an irregular sac consisting of two ill-defined lobes called the sacculus and the utriculus. This system is filled with fluid. From the sac a thin tube extends dorsally to open on the top of the head. In living vertebrates this open tube – the ductus endolymphaticus – is unique to sharks. In most vertebrates the ductus endolymphaticus terminates as a closed sac. The function of this structure in sharks is unknown. The semicircular canals and their common sac constitute the inner ear.

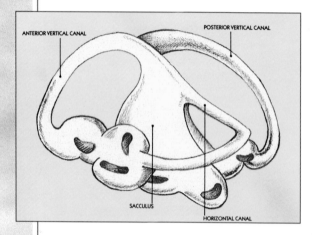

Inside the inner ear are special cells sensitive to movement. The structure of these cells is of great importance to sharks because the same type of cell occurs elsewhere within the sensory systems – most especially in the lateralis system where the 'distant touch' is effected. The body of the cell is fixed in the lining of the inner ear. Free to move in the liquid of the semicircular canals system are minute 'hairs' whose tips are embedded in a solid mass of a gelatinous substance called the cupula. It is the movement of the cupula relative to the cell that gives the brain the information necessary for the fish to orientate itself. As the sensory cells are stimulated by the movement of the body of the fish they are also susceptible to being moved by external factors, especially vibration (which is easily transmitted through liquids). Vibration is the means by which sound waves are transmitted and travel.

Experiments have shown that sharks are particularly sensitive to low-frequency sounds which, in the sea, can travel long distances. The Bull shark, *Carcharinus leucas*, was shown to be sensitive to sounds between 100 and 1500 cycles per second, a part of the middle range of human hearing. Different species of shark are sensitive to different sound ranges and comparative anatomical studies on sharks' ears have suggested that predatory sharks have a more acute sense of hearing than less predatory sharks.

The sense of 'distant touch' relies on cells that work on the same principle as the cupula-bearing cells (neuromasts) of the internal ear. The lateral line system, the 'lateralis', consists of a series of subcutaneous canals or tubes, filled with fluid and well provided with neuromasts.

The canals usually open to the exterior through small pores; a structure in which the canals are completely open (ie trough-like) is thought to represent the primitive condition and is now present only in the Frilled shark *Chlamydoselachus*. The lateral line runs the length of the side of the body and branches over the head.

Vibrations – corresponding to pressure changes – are detected by the lateral line, and it is this detection that has led to the sense being called 'distant touch'. A blinded shark can soon locate a disturbance in the water with remarkable accuracy, and can also avoid collisions with stationary objects. This valuable attribute is very closely related to hearing, for both hearing and 'distant touch' rely on the pressure-change detectors – the neuromasts with their cupulae.

In addition to their organized mass presence within the lateralis canals, free, isolated neuromasts are scattered over the body surface.

VISION

Despite a persistent misconception, sharks' eyesight is good – as experiments on captive sharks have shown. Sharks can adjust their pupils to compensate for changes in light intensity; constriction of the pupil in bright light is more rapid than dilation of the pupil in dim light. The arrangement and numerical ratio of the two types of light-receiving cells (rods and cones) in the retina shows that sharks have a poor sense of colour but have excellent visual acuity for moving objects and in dim light. The ability to

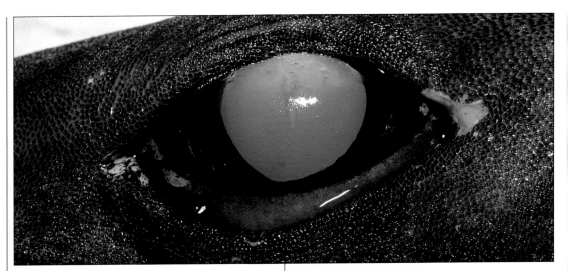

Left ■ The eye of the gulper shark *Centrophorus granulosus*. Research has shown that many species can hunt by sight and, in fact, have excellent vision.

fully utilize low levels of light comes about because of the tapetum – a layer behind the retina that reflects light which has already passed through the retina back into it again. Whereas this is a useful adaptation in dim light, in bright light the shark could be dazzled and rendered temporarily sightless. To prevent this, each of the silvery platelets that form the tapetum is covered with cells containing dark pigment. In bright light the pigment spreads out across the platelet and reduces the amount of light reflected back into the retina. Sharks that always live in deep water lack this 'sunglasses' mechanism. Deep-water sharks also have a different light-sensitive pigment in their retinal cells – a pigment that is especially sensitive to the wavelength of the blue light that penetrates furthest into the sea.

Some sharks – particularly the larger, carnivorous species – have a nictitating membrane (a third eyelid) that comes across the eye to protect it when the shark is biting. Such sharks are thus unable to see their prey for the last second or two before biting it.

OTHER SENSES

Although there are reports of unpalatable objects recovered from sharks' stomachs (old tyres, pieces of wood, etc.), a shark's sense of taste is keen. Many observations have been made of a shark taking an object into its mouth and, on finding it tastes unpleasant, rejecting it. The Moses sole relies on the relative delicacy of the shark's sense of taste for its survival, having developed a chemical repellent that is revolting to shark taste-buds.

Above ■ The pattern of pores on the snout of this bonnethead mark the sites of the electroreceptive ampullae of Lorenzini.

Under the skin on the snout of a shark there is an elaborate arrangement of small gelatinous organs. These are the ampullae of Lorenzini, named to honour the Italian anatomist Stefano Lorenzini who described these organs in 1678. Externally, the ampullae of Lorenzini are marked by a pattern of pores on the snout. Not until about 50 years ago was the function of the ampullae known. Then it was noticed that some dogfish in captivity were sensitive to weak electric fields. They were seen consistently

While odour stimuli are thought to attract a shark to potential prey from a distance, at close quarters sharks can pin-point targets by detecting weak electrical stimuli created by muscular movements in the prey.

Left ■ Remoras have a disc on the tops of their heads with which they can attach themselves to a shark – or any other large fish – by vacuum action. The relationship is not symbiotic: the remora gets free travel and free snacks, the shark seems to get nothing. The disc is a highly modified dorsal fin in which the lateral halves of each ray have been separated and lie across the top of the head.

to avoid a piece of rusty iron but made no attempt to avoid similarly-shaped non-electrogenic objects. It was also known that some rays had similar propensities. The surgical removal of the nerve from the ampullae of Lorenzini, showed that the organ was the site of electroreception.

The ampullae are extremely sensitive, the stimulation threshold being about one microvolt (one millionth of a volt). As the electrical potential produced by such an insignificant act as the gill movements of a flat fish is over 1,000 microvolts per centimetre, the shark is well able to locate any fish going about its ordinary business. It is this remarkable sensitivity that has led to suggestions that sharks attack boats and divers' cages because of the electrical fields they produce. The importance of this ability is greater for deep-sea sharks. In one set of experiments, large carnivorous sharks were shown to be more attracted to an electrode than to the odour of chopped-up fish.

It has also been suggested that sharks may be able to use the earth's magnetic field for navigational purposes.

As if the array of known senses was not enough, there is still one more organ whose function is not known. This is the spiracular organ, a blind tube that lies in front of the gills. It is innervated by a branch of the lateral nerve and lined with sensory ciliary cells – but what the cells detect remains a mystery.

We cannot ever know precisely what use a shark makes of its senses, but we can guess. Sound, especially low-frequency sound, can travel long distances in water: sharks may be able to perceive a sound emanating some kilometres away. The sense of smell, allowing for such variable factors as dilution and current speed, may become effective within some hundreds of metres of the source. Sight probably becomes usefully involved at a lesser distance – clarity of the water and depth are important limiting factors. The neuromasts may well be activated at distances of tens of metres, whereas electroreception seems to be most efficient at closer range. Almost at the point of contact with the source, taste is engaged, giving a shark a final chance to reject the possible food item. Lastly, and by definition a sense of contact, is touch.

CHAPTER THREE

SHARK REPRODUCTION

The Horn shark, *Heterodontus francisci,* derives its common name from the ridges above its eyes. Most Horn (or Bullhead) sharks lay their eggs in amazingly shaped spiral egg cases (see following page).

All sharks practise internal fertilization. It was once thought, as may still be seen in some books, that the Greenland shark, *Somniosus*, was an exception and that its eggs were fertilized externally, but this is now known not to be true.

The pelvic fins of the male are modified into intromittent organs called claspers. Apart from the obvious presence of claspers in the male, other external sexual differences (secondary sexual characteristics) are present in some species. It is not uncommon for females to be larger than males; an extreme case is seen in *Iago omanensis*, in which the male is only two-thirds the length of the female and may weigh only one-sixth as much. The reverse size difference is rare; one such exception, however, is *Holohalaelurus punctatus*, in which the male is larger than the female. Another sexual difference, related to mating behaviour, is exemplified by (among others) *Leptocharias smithi*, the males of which have much larger teeth than the female. In species showing this feature, the skin is much thickened behind the female's head and from the position of scars, it is reasonably deduced that the male holds the female by the neck during copulation and her thickened skin precludes any serious damage from the male's larger teeth.

Generally, very little is known about reproduction in sharks. It seems to be fairly common for sociable species to pass a large part of their adult life in unisex groups and to meet members of the opposite sex only during a mating phase. Scientific ignorance of this aspect of shark life is not surprising. Only a minority of species have been seen alive in their natural habitat, and the chance of observing a transitory activity like mating is remote. Few sharks survive well in captivity, and even fewer have given birth or been seen mating under these conditions.

Within sharks there are three reproductive strategies, each of which represents an increase in the protection afforded to the unborn young over and above the indiscriminate scattering and external fertilization of the eggs. These three strategies are oviparous, ovoviviparous and viviparous, which may be defined as follows:

1. *Oviparous* sharks lay eggs with a leathery shell. The young develop inside the egg-case and are fed by their yolk sac.

EGG CASES

The shapes of egg cases laid by oviparous sharks are species-specific. Members of the Bullhead shark family, for example, lay spiral, flanged cases which the mother carefully wedges into rock crevices to avoid predation (bottom). Compare the much simpler egg case of the Dogfish.

2. *Ovoviviparous* sharks: the egg shell is only weakly formed and the young soon hatch inside the mother, are nourished by their yolk sac, and are not born until this is used up.

3. *Viviparous* sharks: there is hardly any development of the egg shell. When the embryo arrives at the uterus, a small yolk sac is at the end of a long 'umbilical cord'. The yolk sac starts to branch and forms a sort of 'yolk placenta'. As the yolk is used up, the relationship between the embryo and the maternal tissues becomes more complex and intimate, and the young are nourished by the food in the maternal blood in a manner analagous to that of mammals. There are slight variations on this theme.

In some species the young are nourished by a secretion produced by the lining of the uterus – 'uterine milk' – rather than by substances dissolved in the mother's blood.

The three reproductive systems, although in themselves stages in an evolutionary continuum, are useful in shark classification and in elucidating shark biology. They are not, however, universally reliable indicators of shark relationships. More than one system may be present within the members of one family and even, in the case of *Galeus arae*, within different populations of the same species.

It can be seen that the greater the degree of embryo care by the mother, the greater is the chance of survival of the offspring. However, after the young have left the mother, whether in the form of an egg or a miniature shark, there is no further maternal care.

An extension of the seeming end-point in embryo care shown by viviparity occurs in the Hammerhead sharks and a few others. In these cases, while still in the uterus, the largest embryos start eating the less developed embryos and eggs.

Although not uncommon in bony fishes, hermaphroditism and sex reversal are not a normal part of shark biology. Sharks are always either male or female for life.

Irrespective of the reproductive strategy, the sex organs of sharks are remarkably uniform and, as is common with vertebrates in general, linked with the urinary excretory system (see page 32).

The eggs are produced in the ovaries. Ovaries are paired, but it is common for only one to be functional. They are elongated pale-coloured organs located either side of the midline towards the front of the abdominal cavity. In the ovaries the spherical yolky eggs can be seen at different stages of development. When mature, ova (whether one or more than one at a time is not known) are released into the body cavity from where they are carried, presumably by ciliary action, into the funnel at the end of the oviduct. The oviduct is, in essence, a long tube that runs backwards to open into the cloaca (the combined genital and excretory opening). A bulge behind the oviduct, often about halfway along, represents the shell gland where, in species that lay eggs, the shell is secreted around the fertilized egg. Stored sperm, necessary to fertilize the egg before it is encased in the shell, are found in front of the

A female Gulper shark *Centrophorus granulosus* giving birth. The foetus emerges through the cloaca, which serves as a combined genital and excretory opening in all sharks.

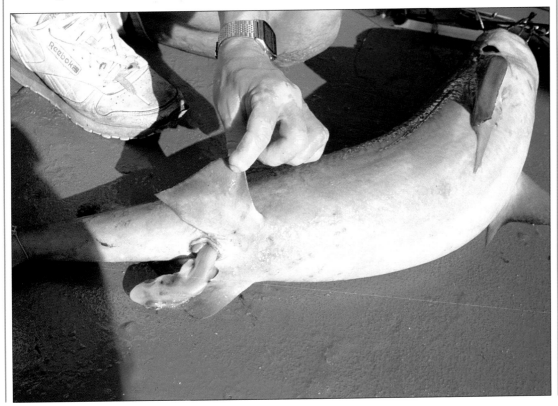

Right ■ Inverting the stomach of a Lemon shark pup under anaesthetic, in order to identify the gut contents; this representative of the species – between one and two years old – was born in the mangrove shallows off Florida. As it matures, it moves into deeper waters and presumably changes its diet accordingly. This change of diet was the central concern of the survey: the researchers confirmed, among other things, that sharks do not eat constantly. Pups like this were found to eat about once every three days.

The claspers of the male shark, illustrated here in 'generalized' form, are extensions of the pelvic fins; (the female skeletal structure is shown above). Each clasper contains a cartilaginous rod. Claspers vary in shape according to species. The developing shark embryo is connected to the yolk sac by a thin stalk. The eyes and gill slits are among the first recognizable features to appear.

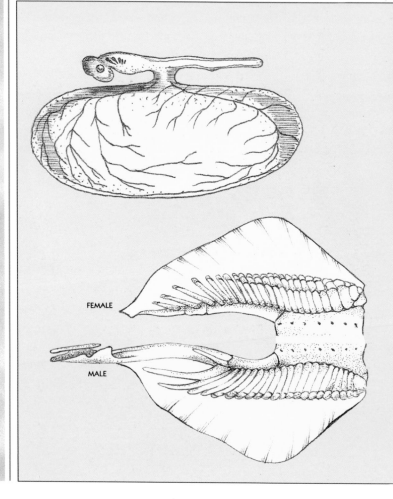

FEMALE

MALE

shell gland. In species that are ovoviviparous or vivi-parous the development of the shell gland is greatly reduced and may be scarcely detectable.

The egg-case shape, and the length and position of the tendrils are characteristic for many species. The eggs are laid in areas where the tendrils may catch on to underwater growths (algae or corals) and be held there until the young hatch. Although there is no parental care as such, female Port Jackson sharks (Heterodontidae) have been seen carrying their spiral-shaped eggs in their mouths and wedging, almost screwing, them into crevices in rocks to pre-vent them from being dislodged.

Gestation periods for ovoviviparous and vivi-parous sharks are, where known, equally prolonged. Indeed, taken as a whole, sharks have the longest gestation periods of any vertebrate group.

In male sharks the testes lie in a position equiva-lent to the ovaries in the female, but the testes are smaller. The sperm produced in them pass poste-riorly through ducts into a capacious seminal vesicle. The paired vesicles open into the male's cloaca. An opening in the cloaca adjacent to that of each seminal vesicle leads into a blind sac usually called the spermatic sac. The precise function of this sac is not known in all species.

Left ■ The embryo of a Porbeagle *Lamna nasus* with a yolk-full belly. This species, in common with a few others, practises a bizarre form of intra-uterine cannibalism known as oophagy. The first embryos to hatch feed on the supply of other eggs as the female continues to ovulate.

The time taken for the eggs to hatch varies greatly between species, and is also affected by water temperature; eggs in colder waters take longer to hatch. In some species the eggs may hatch in a few months, whereas up to two years' gestation has been reported for the Spiny dogfish *Squalus acan-thias*. When the yolk sac has been used up, the young break free of the egg-case. Vigorous wriggling is usually sufficient for them to escape the egg, but in the scyliorhinid *Cephaloscyllium ventriosum* from the western Pacific, the young have two rows of sharp, enlarged denticles on the head to help them penetrate the egg-case.

In at least some species, sperm are formed into packets, called spermatophores, before insertion into the female. These have been graphically described by Gavin Maxwell, who observed a har-pooned Basking shark ejaculating. He wrote: '. . . He emitted a great quantity of what we afterwards found to be sperm. It was not a fluid, but hundreds of semi-opaque milky globules like golf balls, vary-ing in size, and looking as though made of Lalique glass.' Subsequent scientific examination of har-pooned male Basking sharks showed that sperm are formed into spermatophores inside the seminal vesicle. The sperm are conducted into small pockets and then rotated into little spheres by cilia while epithelial cells secrete the clear coating around them. Several gallons of spermatophores are present in a male *Cetorhinus*. Presumably, the coating is dissolved inside the female to release the sperm for fertilization of the egg when needed. The protective coat must also play an important part in the storage of sperm thought to occur inside the female.

Sperm are transferred to the female by the male's claspers. The sperm pass from the cloaca into the oviduct where fertilization occurs.

Copulation in sharks is poorly known to science. Claspers are erectile – an observation noted in some live sharks and produced experimentally by using the hormone adrenaline (epinephrine) or by electrical stimulation of the appropriate spinal nerve. For most species it is not known if one or both claspers are used. There are some sharks, in fact, in which only one clasper can be used because each one of the pair is too distant from its partner to be inserted. It has been argued that only one clasper may be used by species in which the female has only one functional ovary.

Copulation has been seen in the Lesser Spotted dogfish (*Scyliorhinus caniculus*). In this elongated, supple species, the male winds completely around the female, who remains immobile but in a normal swimming position. This method could not be practised by many of the larger sharks, for the body of the male is too stocky to entwine around the female. In one stockier species, *Heterodontus franciscii*, copulation was observed when a pair were in captivity in the Steinhart Aquarium, San Francisco. The male was slightly smaller than the female (not uncommon in sharks) and held her left pectoral fin in his mouth. Holding on to this fin, the male twisted

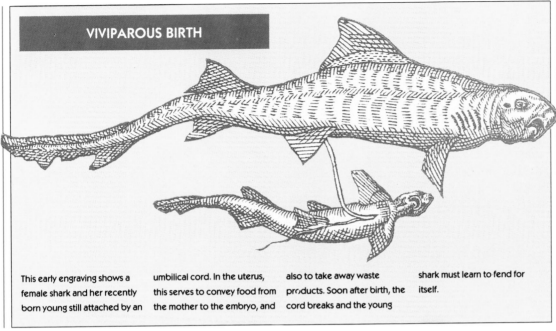

VIVIPAROUS BIRTH

This early engraving shows a female shark and her recently born young still attached by an umbilical cord. In the uterus, this serves to convey food from the mother to the embryo, and also to take away waste products. Soon after birth, the cord breaks and the young shark must learn to fend for itself.

Opposite, Below ■ The cloaca of a young female bonnethead. Not surprisingly, sharks very quickly become distressed when taken from the water: this pink flush is an early sign, together with a blotchiness in the grey top side. It was definitely time to release this specimen.

Below ■ For copulation to take place in the Lesser Spotted dogfish *Scyliorhinus caniculus*, the male must completely wind around the female.

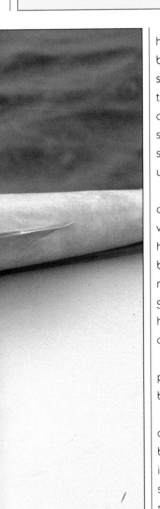

his body around so that his tail lay over the female's back between her dorsal fins. Then, he used her second dorsal fin as a fixed point against which to thrust and was able to place his clasper into her cloaca. During this time the female remained passive. Observations of subsequent matings of this species revealed that only the right clasper was used.

Lemon Sharks (*Negaprion brevirostris*) have been observed mating at night in captivity. The process was described thus: 'The sharks were side by side, heads slightly apart but the posterior parts of their bodies in such close contact and the swimming movements so perfectly synchronized that they gave the appearance of a single individual with two heads, as they swam in slow counterclockwise circles around the pen.'

It is possible that the 'swimming in tandem' phenomenon, noted in Basking sharks may in reality be instances of these animals mating.

Overall, very little is known about shark courtship or mating. Some species tend to live in unisex groups, but what factors cause the break-up of these groups into mating couples is unknown. In some species of sharks, the males do not eat at all during the mating phase, a phenomenon that doubtless ensures the survival of the females held by the males' jaws during copulation.

CHAPTER FOUR

SHARKS THROUGH HISTORY

A 2.2m (7ft) long Whitetip Reef
shark *Triaenodon obesus*
cruising over reef flat.

Below ■ Fossil shark teeth; it has been estimated that over the span of just a few years some sharks may grow, utilize and then discard tens of thousands of teeth. It is therefore not surprising that shark teeth are probably the world's most common vertebrate fossils.

It is only in the last two centuries that sharks have in general had a bad press. And yet there seems to be no good reason for such a historically recent fear of sharks, nor, indeed, is there any justification for their maleficent reputation. After all, the gory details published in books, and dramatized or fictionalized on the screen, have had no cautionary effect – people still go swimming. Rather the opposite effect has been achieved: people have to some extent sought confrontations with sharks, with the result that such confrontations have occasionally been to the detriment of the swimmers but have far more commonly been to the detriment of the sharks, some species of which are now rare. In recent decades, moreover, the rarity of such species has been occasioned as much by selective hunting, for human profit and short-term glory, as by pollution.

Aristotle, who lived in the 4th century BC, was the first naturalist to record that *Selache* (as he called sharks) and the rays had cartilaginous skeletons. It was he who wrote about the mouths of sharks that '... it is placed on the undersurface so that these fishes turn on the back in order to take their food', and thus started a misconception that persisted for over two millennia – that sharks turn on their back to feed.

Although we have no reason to assume that sharks have changed their dietary habits in the past two thousand years, the early writers made no mention of humans having been eaten. Either such an event was regarded as so normal as to be not worth mentioning or the occasion very rarely arose for it to happen.

Oppian's *Halieutics on the Nature of Fish* was written in Greek during the 2nd century AD. It was not, however, until 1722 that an English translation rescued this charming work from academic obscurity. The rhyming couplets of the translation describe the White shark thus:

'White sharks the Fisher's Curse, force on their Way
And ominous Hyaena's size their prey'

The only major note of danger or malice on sharks in it, however, occurs in a general passage referring to teeth:

> Who see the Shark's capacious Jaws disclose
> A thousand tusks erect in flaming rows
> Dispise the tuskèd Boar.

Left ■ Weird and wonderful mythical sea creatures abound on the pages of old natural histories. The exaggerated tales of seafarers would have had much to do with what the artist eventually depicted in his drawings.

Magellan, describing his journey round the world between 1519 and 1522, noted that while his ship was delayed in the doldrums off the west coast of Africa, sharks (*Tiburoni*) swam around it. He said that they had terrible teeth and ate men when the found them, dead or alive. In the same paragraph, Magellan noted how to catch them and stated that they were not good to eat.

In the middle of the 16th century, Guillaume Rondelet, a professor of medicine at Montpellier University, published the first eyewitness account of a shark consuming human flesh. Rondelet wrote of the Great White shark (he called it *La Lamie* after the Greek mythological flesh-eating monster): 'This fish eats others; it is very greedy, it devours men whole, as I know from experience: for between Nice and Marseilles, where *Lamies* are sometimes caught, in a stomach has been found a human body with full armour.' From this 'observation' and from other stomach contents noted, Rondelet concluded that there was no reason it should not have been a Great White shark that swallowed Jonah, rather than a whale. (Parenthetically, even if the record of the body encased in armour is an exaggeration, it is noteworthy that some sharks do appear to delay the digestion of food.)

The word 'shark' itself does not appear to have been printed before 1569, when it was used by sailors of Sir John Hawkins' Caribbean Expedition who brought one back for exhibition in London. Prior to that time sharks had been known in English by their Spanish name, 'Tiburon'.

Two incidents vie for the title of the earliest authenticated record of shark attack; earlier reports are uncorroborated and lack supporting detail. One was in 1749 when a 14-year-old orphan, Brook Watson, had his right leg removed below the knee. Such an accident had no deleterious effect on Master Watson's career, he became an MP in 1784 and Lord Mayor of London in 1796. The amputated leg even formed a part of Watson's coat of arms when he became a baronet in 1803. Apart from using his wooden leg for his personal advantage, he further capitalized on the shark attack by commissioning a painting of the incident from the American artist John Copley in 1778. This painting was exhibited at the Royal Academy in that year, where its accuracy

(or lack of it) caused a great deal of controversy. Although painted about 30 years after the incident, by an artist who had seen neither Havana harbour nor a shark, recent authorities have tentatively identified the shark as a Tiger shark.

The other shark attack, seemingly based on reality, appears in Thomas Percy's *Reliques of Ancient English Poetry*, published in 1775. There, in a ballad entitled *Bryan and Pereen – a West Indian Ballad*, are the deathless lines:

Then through the white surf did she haste
To clasp her lovely swain,
When ah! a shark bit through his waist:
His heart's blood dyed the main!

He shrieked! his half sprang from the wave,
Streaming with purple gore,
And soon it found a living grave,
And ah! was seen no more.

An explanatory preamble to the ballad informs that it 'is founded on a real fact, that happened in the island of St Christopher's about two years ago. The editor owes the following stanzas to the friendship of Dr James Grainger who was in the island when this tragical accident happened, and is now an eminent physician there.' The date is uncertain but is reckoned to be either about 1730 or about 1760. There is no doubt, however, that Dr Grainger really existed.

More modern newspaper accounts may have one advantage over the older versions of similar incidents. They often have photographs, taken at the time, rather than engravings made from verbal descriptions which inevitably fixed the inaccuracies for evermore. But even today, with photographs provided, the more sensational stories exaggerate the size of the shark, in the certain knowledge that very few people are going to try and work out the size of the shark from the objects around it in the photograph. As an American shark expert, the late Dr Gudger, wrote 'all fishes shrink under the tape measure'.

An example of this exaggeration concerns Dr Gudger's difficulties in obtaining an exact measurement of a specific shark. On 14 May, 1933, the Italian vessel *Francesco Crispi* was near the mid-point of the west coast of the Red Sea. About 9pm a dull

Left ■ Great White sharks can be caught by rod-and-line, by nets or by harpooning them. When one is brought ashore, it's bound to cause a stir. This specimen, by no means the largest ever landed, tipped the scales at 1,040kg (2,300lb). Small wonder when contemplating such a catch, that sharks have captured the imagination for centuries, inspiring terror and even hatred. On a voyage in 1593 Sir Richard Hawkins – the first person to bring a shark back to England – observed that the sailors would daily capture and torture sharks: 'They live long, and suffer much after they bee taken, before they dye.'

Right ■ An early anatomical drawing of the underside of a shark. The accuracy of such studies must remain in doubt: the mouth here appears surprisingly small and the pectoral fins look more like a penguin's flippers.

thud was heard at the bow of the ship and its speed dropped. At first light a large shark was seen doubled around the leading edge of the ship and held fast there by water pressure. The shark was hauled aboard and the ship continued to its destination of Massawa in what was then Eritrea, Italian Somaliland. In 1934, Dr Gudger received a cutting from a German newspaper from a correspondent in Havana, Cuba. This showed a Whale shark hung up at the side of the vessel *Francesco Crispi*. Although a port was visible in the background, no locality was given. The article did, however, state that the shark was about 12 metres long. No further details were forthcoming.

Time, coincidence and luck came to Dr Gudger's rescue when after two entire years his enquiries about the shark had not provided the information he wanted. In 1936, he came across an article written by Professor Santucci of Genoa describing the Whale shark whose details Gudger had been trying to find. By luck, Professor Santucci had been in Massawa when the *Francesco Crispi*, with its unusual and unexpected cargo, docked. He had also been given the opportunity to make external and internal mea-

surements on the shark, and was thus able to illustrate the exaggeration of the newspapers in alleging the fish's length to be 12 metres (39ft). It was in truth only 7.4 metres (24ft) long.

Such exaggeration of size is not confined to sharks. The fish that the angler says he has lost is traditionally always bigger than the one that actually did escape. (Perhaps every fish's motive in evading capture is to grow into one of the size that the angler wants it to be!) Any headline writer will know, of course, that 'Man-eating shark terrorizes Californian surfers' will be more attractive than 'A Great White Shark, somewhat confused, has been mistaking surfers for sealions, its normal food.'

BASKING SHARKS AND
SEA SERPENTS

The sea serpent (or serpents) is a long-enduring, so far unestablished, product of wish-fulfilment. Sightings have never been corroborated. Many are no doubt misidentifications made by honest people; others are the result purely of the imagination of sensation-seekers. The sceptics say 'Provide a corpse or a good photograph and the mystery will be solved.' Well, there have been some corpses and some good photographs of those corpses. All, so far, have been of the plesiosaur-type of sea serpent – the long-necked small-headed variety likened to the extinct aquatic reptile.

Parenthetically, it should be noted that crypto-zoologists (people who specialize in unknown animals) divide sea-serpent sightings into several categories, each supposedly referring to one 'species'. These categories correspond to descriptions such as long-necked, merhorse, many-humped, many-finned, super-otter, super-eel, and so on.

Certain sightings and strandings, because of the presence of a corpse and/or photographs, have taken on an air of unjustified authenticity in the annals of less responsible cryptozoological studies. These include the Stronsa beast of 1808, the Henry Island monster of 1934, the Querquerville monster also of 1934, the Hendaye carcase of 1951, and the New South Wales carcase of 1960. The initial descriptions

of these carcases incorporated such phrases as 'paddle-like front legs', 'four legs', 'fur or fleece', 'long-necked', and 'winged'.

Subsequent expert examination of the photographs, drawings, or the actual corpses proved that all were the remains of Basking sharks. Although this identification was beyond doubt in these cases, many supporters of sea serpents have refused to believe, or have chosen to ignore, these determinations. Their usual response has been that the long-necked corpse could not be the remains of a Basking shark because that animal does not have a long neck. Although that statement is true, it is the interpretation put upon the series of vertebrae identified as the neck that has been wrong.

The solution to the problem is simple if the nature of the Basking shark's skeleton is known. The skull of the Basking shark, or at least the part that houses the brain and the orbits (the cranium), is very small. The extensive gill slits – those great slashes at the sides of the throat that almost divide the shark in two – are vital to allow the vast quantities of food-carrying water through the shark's sieving system. When the shark dies and begins to rot, there is very little muscle in the gill region to decay. Consequently, the gill area – then the big jaws – soon separate from the rest of the corpse. The anterior half-dozen vertebrae are then left supporting the small cranium – resulting in what looks like a long neck supporting a small head with eye sockets. Behind the gill area is the pectoral fin skeleton, probably with the partly decomposed pectoral fins still present. Hence the 'paddle-like front legs'. The 'wings' are the rods that compose the gill arches themselves (should any still be left). The 'fur' or 'fleece' is the partly decomposed muscle. If you have ever eaten in a British fish and chip shop what is called rock salmon, huss or dogfish, you will have eaten a small species of shark. You may also have noticed that the flesh is more fibrous than the flesh of cod or haddock. It is the partly decomposed flesh of the much larger Basking shark that presents an even 'hairier' appearance than that of the fried huss. Hence the misinterpretation of the coarse muscle fibres as hair or fur.

So, so far, all 'sea serpent' corpses have been those of the no less remarkable *Cetorhinus maximus* – the Basking shark.

Below Left ■ Could this have been the fish that Jonah ended up inside? The temperate-water Basking shark is only surpassed in size by the Whale shark – another plankton feeder – but one confined to the world's tropical oceans.

CHAPTER FIVE

SHARK ATTACK

Valerie Taylor testing an anti-shark mesh suit (called a 'neptunic') with the help of a 2m Blue shark in deep water off the coast of California. The suit consists of approximately 400,000 stainless steel rings which prevent penetration by shark teeth, though considerable bruising can result from a bite.

A feeding frenzy of Grey Reef sharks *Carcharinus amblyrhynchos,* stimulated by leaving bait (in this case dead fish) tied to the top of a rock outcrop. In situations like this, nearby divers and underwater photographers may well get bitten inadvertently in the melee, and the sharks will also attack each other.

Sharks do attack humans. They also attack, and eat, seals, sea-lions, birds, turtles, fish, crustaceans, shellfish and plankton. Circumstantial evidence – eg teeth marks and stomach contents – shows that they could be accused of attacking, and eating, under-sea cables, sea anchors, small boats, oil drums, sea-weed, planks of wood, old tyres, beer cans . . . and other sharks.

Yes, sharks do attack humans – but it is important to put such relatively rare events in perspective and to realize that sharks do not single out the human species as the object of a vicious predetermined vendetta. The interaction between sharks and humans is the same as that between sharks and any other floating or swimming object that attracts their attention. But human self-centeredness rarely appreciates this. If a shark bites and eats a seal, that is fine (except for the seal). If a shark eats another shark that is even better. But if a shark bites a human, the shark is promptly branded as a savage killer deliberately attempting to slaughter peaceful bathers and surfers who are just enjoying themselves in the sea. It is also quite acceptable for us to eat shark meat, but not for the shark to eat human flesh.

Although the phrase 'shark attack' is commonly employed to describe shark-human interaction, the use of the word 'attack' could in reality be mislead-ing because of its overtly antagonistic implications. 'Enemy' is usually linked with 'attack', one does not, however, attack enemies with the motive of eating them. Thus it is with sharks: their 'motive' is food, not an all-out assault on *Homo sapiens.* Despite this, the phrase 'shark attack' remains in frequent use.

There are about 350 species of sharks – but fewer than 30 species have been known to attack humans. During the period 1958 to 1967, all known reports of shark attacks were collected, collated and filed by a group of scientists and other interested parties under the auspices of the US Navy. Although the list of attacks extended back into historical times, the great majority were recorded after the end of World War II. (Hardly any were logged during the War possibly because the usual medical report listed wounds that perhaps should have been attributed to sharks as 'unspecified animal bites'.) Of the reports gathered during the period that the survey was in progress, about 500 recorded attacks could

not be used for pattern analysis because the data were so sparse that the analysts could not always even be certain if the attack was real. Finally, nearly 1,200 reports were used in the computer analysis to try to find the answers to why, where and how attacks occur, and what species were most commonly involved. The results were enlightening.

First, shark attacks are rare, and only some 30% of the people bitten die. Death is mostly due to loss of blood and shock, which can result in the victim's drowning before rescue. Instances of a shark eating any substantial portion of a human prey are very few. It seems that sharks actually do not like human flesh.

Most bites, as might be expected, are on the lower part of the legs, from the knees downwards; thighs are the next most vulnerable part of the body, followed by the arms, middle of the trunk, chest, back, shoulders. Least attacked of all is the head. In other words, most attacks are directed towards the rear part of the swimmer. The hands and arms seem mostly to be bitten when the victim tries to fend off the shark. The most frequent wounds are deep lacerations, as if the taste of the preliminary bite is enough to tell the shark it has chosen the wrong sort of food. Occasionally the flesh may be stripped from the long bones of the limbs or from the ribcage. A large, sharp bite may expose the intestines. It is rare for much human flesh or appendages to be swallowed, and even rarer for a large part, or the whole, of a corpse to be ingested.

In considering a shark's consumption of food it is worth noting that some observations suggest that sharks can, in some way, delay the digestion of food. Sometimes, when caught or when sick, sharks have been known to regurgitate the contents of their sto-machs. Among the collection of objects so dis-carded it has been noted that parts of carcases may show different degrees of having been digested. One particularly important observation came from a Tiger shark (*Galeocerdo cuvieri*) which had been kept for about a month at Taronga Park Zoo in Sydney, Australia. A few times in captivity it had been fed on horse meat, which it spewed out after having swallowed. It died after a month, and the autopsy revealed two undigested dolphins in its stomach which could only have been consumed before it

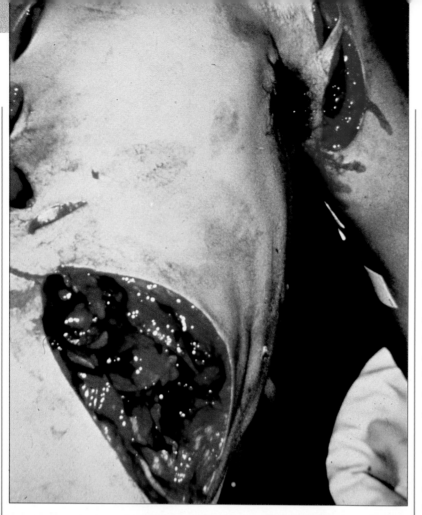

was captured. How this mechanism works is un-known. It may be that some types of flesh are less digestible in the stomach of particular species of shark. It may be that the shark can, in some way, stop or reduce the production of digestive fluids. (How-ever, the fact that sharks can delay digesting their food is not sufficient evidence to substantiate the suggestion made by some authors that Jonah was swallowed not by a whale but by a Great White shark.)

Statistics can be used spuriously to prove almost anything, and this is especially true for statistics on shark attacks. Apart from the fact that more people are struck by lightning than are bitten by sharks each year, drowning near a bathing beach is more than one thousand times more likely than being killed by a shark around the coasts of the USA.

The computerized statistics for 1958–1967 were also analysed in an attempt to discover if one colour of diving suit is more likely to attract sharks than another colour. Are, for example, stripes more attractive to sharks? Previous observations, and

more recent tests with captive sharks, have shown that sharks have no particular preference for a colour beyond the general rule that they are more likely to investigate a conspicuously bright object rather than a dull one.

Where do sharks attack? The answer is almost everywhere. The attack recorded the farthest north was one off the north of Scotland. In this case, however, the attack took place on board a fishing boat when a small shark was hauled up in a trawl full of fish.

Most shark attacks occur in warm waters at temperatures of about 70°F (21°C). Some authorities believe this to be because the sharks are commoner, and more active, at these temperatures. Other authorities argue that it is because there are more people in the sea in warmer climates. Both, of course, make sense. Throughout the world, shark incidents are relatively numerous off east and south-east Australia and the Pacific islands; the Caribbean and both seaboards of the USA; the Persian Gulf; and, with decreasing frequency, south and east Asia, the Mediterranean and South America.

The distribution of shark attacks must, though, be interpreted with great care. For example, there are very many more reports from the eastern coast of South Africa than from the western coast. This is probably because the western coast is lapped by the cold Benguela current, so fewer people are in the sea. Off the west coast of the USA most attacks are close to large centres of population because (a) there are more swimmers, and (b) the attacks are more likely to be reported. Very few attacks have been recorded from South America, probably because attacks in isolated areas are not reported or because reports in non-European languages are less accessible. Overall, the reported locations of shark attack show little more than where there are concentrations of European-language speakers in the sea and not where there is an abundance of particularly inquisitive sharks.

The timing of shark attacks throughout the year varies from place to place and leads to what are again obvious conclusions. For instance, around New Zealand no attacks have been reported between April and November. That span of months represents New Zealand winter and few people go

swimming in the cold seas. Similarly on the east coast of the USA about 80% of shark attacks occur during the five warmest months (May to September) of the year.

On a smaller timescale, there are more attacks at weekends than on weekdays. During the day, there is a late morning peak, a trough in attacks at lunchtime, and another peak between 2 and 4 pm. Surveys of the human population show that these times are again when most bathers are in the water.

The species of shark most often cited in attacks are, naturally, the larger carnivorous sharks. Of these, three species have claimed most victims: the Great White shark (at least 32 deaths), the Tiger shark (27) and the Bull shark, *Carcharinus leucas* (21).

The proportion of shark attacks in different depths of water has also been analysed. As before, beyond providing information that corresponds to the presence of humans there is little of significance about shark behaviour to be gleaned from the data. Nearly two-thirds of the attacks happened in water less than 1.5m (5ft) deep, while only 1% took place in water more than 45m (150ft) deep. Very similar figures apply to the data recording distance from the shore. One-third of the attacks occurred less than 15m (50ft) from the shore and just 3% from 45–60m (150–200ft) out. All that these statistics reflect is the abundance of people. More people are in shallow water near the shore than in deep

Left ◼ A gruesome photo of Australian diver Rodney Fox's gaping wounds after an attack. He was fortunate to live to tell the tale, chiefly because the shark bit once and then let go. It is thought by some that 50–75% of all shark attacks are not motivated by hunger, although an alternative explanation is that the shark rejects the human victim after the first taste.

Above ◼ Regarded as the most dangerous shark in tropical waters, the Tiger shark *Galeocerdo cuvier* is a known man-eater which may grow to 6m. The more usual items of its diet are bony fish, other sharks, rays, turtles, sea snakes and garbage from ships.

Left ◼ Probably the most widely-known of all sharks, and certainly the most dangerous in temperate waters, the Great White *Carcharodon carcharias* is seen here taking tuna bait from a boat off the South Australian coast.

offshore water. Water clarity has little effect on sharks. Roughly half the attacks were in clear water and the rest were in opaque water.

So far, all the factors influencing the location of shark attack are related more closely to human density than to anything else. There is, however, one statistic that is not quite so simply explained. More than a dozen male humans are attacked for every female – the ratio is about 13.5:1. A census of the beach population shows that males and females are present in roughly equal proportions. Very slightly more males than females go into the water. Males, being physically stronger than females, tend to swim out further and dive deeper than females, but the tendency seems to be far too small to account for the difference in the numbers of each sex attacked. To date there has been no adequate explanation of this phenomenon.

It is not just at sea that sharks attack. Although sharks are essentially marine fishes, at least two species enter freshwater for a time. One of these is the Bull shark (*Carcharinus leucas*), noted above as taking third position in the league table of attacks on humans. The Bull shark has been responsible for attacks in rivers. The attack most distant from the sea was made by a Bull shark nearly 100 miles (160km) up the Karum river in Iran. The same species has been noted in the upper reaches of the Amazon more than 3,200km (2,000 miles) from the sea, but in that region of poor communication any attacks have gone unrecorded. There have also been attacks in freshwater rivers just south of New York (the Matawan Creek attacks of 1916 have a well-known and documented history) and in the Mississippi river.

The overall conclusion from the data so assiduously gathered and analysed is that if humans and sharks are in the same small volume of water at the same time there is the risk of an attack. Such a risk, however, is minute.

If a person is determined to swim in tropical waters, what can be done to minimize the risk of shark attack? There are no really efficient repellents. One little flat fish, the Moses sole, *Pardachirus marmoratus*, secretes a milky fluid that deters sharks from eating it. For the Moses sole the repellent is very effective but, like all repellents, is impractical to use to protect a human diver. The poison simply

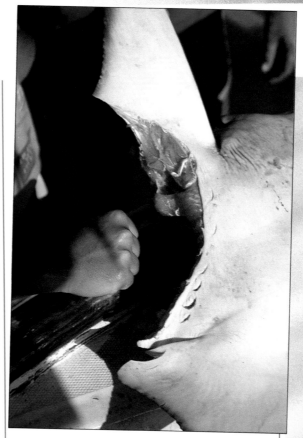

disperses too rapidly in the sea to remain in effective concentrations. It has been calculated that over 2kg (4½lb) of the vital ingredient of the Moses sole secretion would have to be released each hour to keep sharks at bay. It works for the sole because the poison is released in the confined area of the shark's mouth and at a high concentration.

In general, the best 'protection' for a swimmer is to reduce the risk. Find out where the sharks are densest and avoid that area. For example, sharks often concentrate around sewage outfalls or where offal is regularly discharged into the water. Avoid areas where people are fishing – the bait may have already attracted sharks. Swim in groups, the larger the number of people in a group, the less chance of any individual being attacked. Keep clear of areas where the depth changes rapidly – ie near a deep channel. Keep an eye open for any signs of unusual behaviour in the fishes of the area. Avoid wearing bright or reflective garments or decorations that could arouse the sharks' curiosity.

Do not become paranoid about being bitten by a shark: the risk is infinitesimally small. Remember: sharks do not really like the taste of human flesh. For the really paranoid the only safe way to avoid becoming a shark's snack is to stay on the beach. There are no recorded attacks on dry land.

Above Left ■ A seven-foot Lemon shark that was attacked by a tiger shark; the tiger took everything as far as the pectorals. It was identified – as sharks are identified in attacks on humans – by the teeth marks.

Opposite ■ This diver, Henri Bource, lost his leg following an attack by a Great White shark. Great Whites feed primarily on marine mammals, and it's possible they may mistake a human floating in the water for a seal, porpoise or small whale.

CHAPTER SIX

SHARK CONSERVATION

Tag and release at the Bahama Banks; this six-foot Nurse shark was tagged in the skin beneath the first dorsal fin. A blood sample was also taken. Tagging exercises like this one, under the direction of Dr Gruber at the University of Miami, are an excellent method of learning more about shark movement and population.

Sharks are quite unreasonably maligned and so persecuted. If human activities did not overlap into their living space there would be no other contact between sharks and humans. Even when we have been their invaders, they have scarcely interfered with the human species; by contrast we have pointlessly slaughtered millions of them. We also pollute their environment – they do not pollute ours.

Sadly, the indifference shown in the past by people to sharks is only very slowly beginning to change. But enlightenment is becoming more widespread. In *Anglers' Mail* – a magazine devoted to anglers' interests – on 15 August, 1987 there was an article criticizing the way sharks were treated. In particular, a 170kg (378lb) porbeagle was shown hanging by its neck. The author wrote, 'The magnificent fish's reward from its captor was to be hung from a gibbet on the quayside while the angler's vanity was satiated by popping flash bulbs.' Even more importantly the author pointed out that if a dead 9kg (20lb) pike were to appear in print, there would have been an outcry because the fish should have been returned to the water . . .

One of the difficulties in fish conservation is human ignorance. Because fish are neither furry nor cuddly, nor anthropomorphically cute, they are regarded as not even animals. Yet they are sentient creatures. The reduction in shark numbers is due almost entirely to our ignorance, ably fostered by sections of the media who perpetuate the myth of the shark as a savage killer with the single-minded desire to eat people. Such a myth is, sadly, rapidly absorbed by a gullible public. Take, for example, the case of the Great White shark – the 'star' of the *Jaws* films.

The Great White shark is now a very rare fish – so rare that it has been proposed for inclusion on CITES Appendix 1, an international convention which would prohibit its capture worldwide. The species has never been very common because it is the ultimate predator in its food chain so, by definition, it is less abundant than its prey. In comparative statistics its small contribution to the shark population is demonstrated by the fact that generally only 27 Great White sharks have been caught for every 100,000 other sharks. Any unnecessary pressure on this 0.027% of the general shark population could therefore lead to its extinction. The species cannot cope with extraneous interference: only because it has no natural predators can it survive.

But the modern 'macho' image of the big-game hunter has encouraged the selective culling of Great Whites all over the world. An individual tooth, mounted as a pendant, can fetch US$200, and a full set of jaws can be acquired for about $4,000.

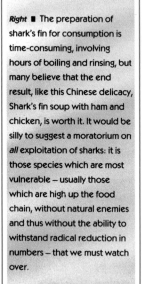

Right ■ The preparation of shark's fin for consumption is time-consuming, involving hours of boiling and rinsing, but many believe that the end result, like this Chinese delicacy, Shark's fin soup with ham and chicken, is worth it. It would be silly to suggest a moratorium on *all* exploitation of sharks: it is those species which are most vulnerable – usually those which are high up the food chain, without natural enemies and thus without the ability to withstand radical reduction in numbers – that we must watch over.

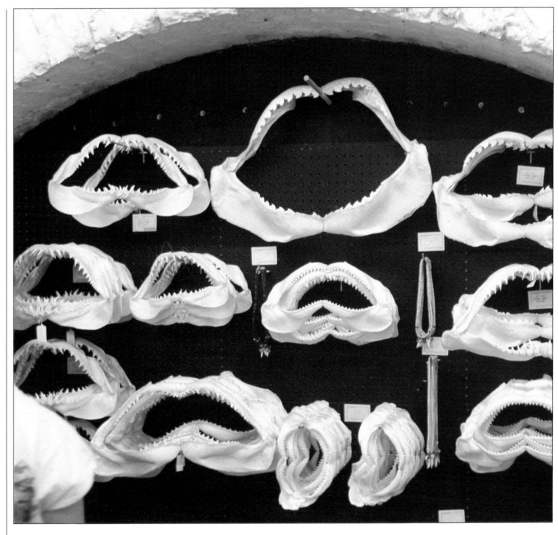

Left ■ Makos (on the left) and bull shark souvenirs, for sale in Key West, Florida; the big pair of jaws are tiger shark. Will souvenirs be all we have left in the years to come?

In the entire western Atlantic, only 76 Great Whites were caught between 1957 and 1983. The story of the film *Jaws* was centred on the Californian coast, where the Great White feeds naturally on sea lions (although most of the location filming was actually carried out off South Australia). One of the main sea lion colonies is on the Falloran Islands off the Californian coast. After four Great Whites had been caught there, all sightings ceased and the sea lion colony proliferated. Because the sea lions are – rightly – a protected species, they began to consume more fish, to the detriment of the local fishermen. Not merely were the fishermen's catches down, but there were reports of sea lions damaging the nets. The natural ecological balance had been disturbed – a situation guaranteed to lead, sooner or later, to some form of penalizing effect on humans.

Off southern Australia the number of Great Whites has fallen dramatically. Rodney Fox, an experienced diver and now one of the champions of the Great White, has reported that only 35 to 40 remain in the area, and that most are virginal males less than 4m (13ft) long. Very few large females have been seen – a situation that does not seem likely to engender a rapid increase in the Great White population. Even if protection were granted now, recovery would be very slow, if it took place at all.

If the possession and display of a set of great white shark jaws confers macho status, the same cannot be said of the possession of any bits of a gentle giant, the Basking shark – the second largest of all fish and by far the largest in European waters. For the drastic reduction in numbers of this species, environmental changes of our making together with commercial hunting must take the blame. This history is worth detailing.

Right ■ The Mako (shown here), Oceanic Blue, Thresher and Great White are highly regarded as fighting fish by game fishermen. It is unfortunate that some fishermen — by no means all — believe that 'the only good shark is a dead shark', regardless of its size or species.

Left ■ A 7m Basking shark hauled up on the slip at the Achill Islands, off Ireland. The liver of such a specimen may be up to 70% of the total body volume, yielding an oil called squalene which is used nowadays in the cosmetics industry and as a lubricant in high altitude aircraft.

COMMERCIAL HUNTING AND SPECIES SURVIVAL: THE BASKING SHARK

Fish oil has been in use for many centuries as a source of light and, latterly, also as a lubricant. For example, the native tribes of British Columbia used to dry an oily, shore-living fish (*Thaleichthys*) and use it as a candle – hence its common name, the candlefish. In the North Atlantic the Basking shark has been hunted for centuries for its oil. An average-sized adult can provide up to 900 litres (200 gallons) of oil from its liver. In isolated coastal areas this was the main source of lamp oil until about the beginning of this century, when cheap mineral oil and easier transportation led to a decline in the primitive fishery.

From about the turn of the century until just after World War II there were no significant catches of Basking sharks for oil. However, the depredations of the war led to the re-utilization of this source of oil on both sides of the Atlantic, especially in the remoter communities. The fish were not hunted just for oil, however. In some areas the flesh was used to make fishmeal fertilizers, the skin was tanned as a very serviceable leather, the cartilage was turned into fish glue, and the fins were dried and used as a basis for soup (so emulating the Chinese shark-fin soup).

Previously, the sharks had been hand-harpooned from small boats, much as whales were hunted in the 18th century. In the resurgent fishery, gun-fired cold (non-explosive) harpoons were used, rather than the explosive harpoons as in whaling, primarily because they were cheaper but also because the brain of a Basking shark is very small and cocooned by fluid in the tiny cartilaginous cranium, and it was argued that the time taken for a shark to die was thus little different whether an explosive harpoon was used or not. In the Achill Islands, off Ireland, the sharks were first caught in extremely strong sisal nets and the trapped animals were then incapacitated by fishermen who severed the spinal cord behind the head with a spear-like implement.

Whether harpooned and dead, or merely incapacitated and prevented from swimming, the leviathans were then lassoed and towed to the shore

Right and Inset ■ The Basking shark fishery on the island of Soay, off the west coast of Scotland, in the late 1940s; once the shark had been harpooned it was pulled to the side of the ship, made fast, and then towed back to harbour.

for appropriate dismemberment. The liver was heated to extract the oil. In the late 1940s, the price of shark liver oil then rose to a rate per ton at which the commercial taking of basking sharks became very much a lucrative – not merely a viable – commercial enterprise.

The shoaling and surface feeding habits of *Cetorhinus* made them an easy prey, with inevitable results: the overall numbers of the fish plummeted. They were being killed faster than they could reproduce. Consider, for example, the figures for the Achill Island fishery from 1950 to 1975.

Achill Island Fishery Statistics		
Year	No. of sharks taken	Tons of oil sold
1950	905	160
1951	1630	375
1952	1808	340
1953	1068	230
1954	1162	270
1955	1708	135
1956	977	190
1957	468	104
1958	500	110
1959	280	70
1960	219	47
1961	258	59
1962	116	20
1963	75	19
1964	39	10
1965	47	12
1966	46	11.5
1967	41	11
1968	75	19
1969	113	29
1970	42	11
1971	29	7
1972	62	15
1973	85	19
1974	33	8.5
1975	38	9

merely been over-exploitation of a discrete local population of Basking sharks, a group that remained in that area of western Ireland, moving into deep water in winter and coming inshore to be available for catching in spring and summer. Reference to more widely based Basking shark catch returns soon proved that the same dramatic fall in numbers was occurring elsewhere.

The European Economic Community and Norwegian statistics combined for 1978–1986 are given below. The numbers of Basking sharks actually caught has been back-calculated from the recorded weight of liver using the figure of 0.5 metric tons of liver per shark. For the last three years of these figures, almost the entire catch was Norwegian.

Sharks caught 1978–1986	
Year	No. of sharks
1978	1563
1979	2266
1980	1570
1981	770
1982	930
1983	759
1984	888*
1985	631*
1986	493*

In the early years of the fishery, the extra income gained by the less than wealthy Achill Islanders was most welcome, it was not long, however, before the revenue plummeted as the number of sharks caught diminished. At first it was thought that there had

*Figures based on the data available at time of going to press.

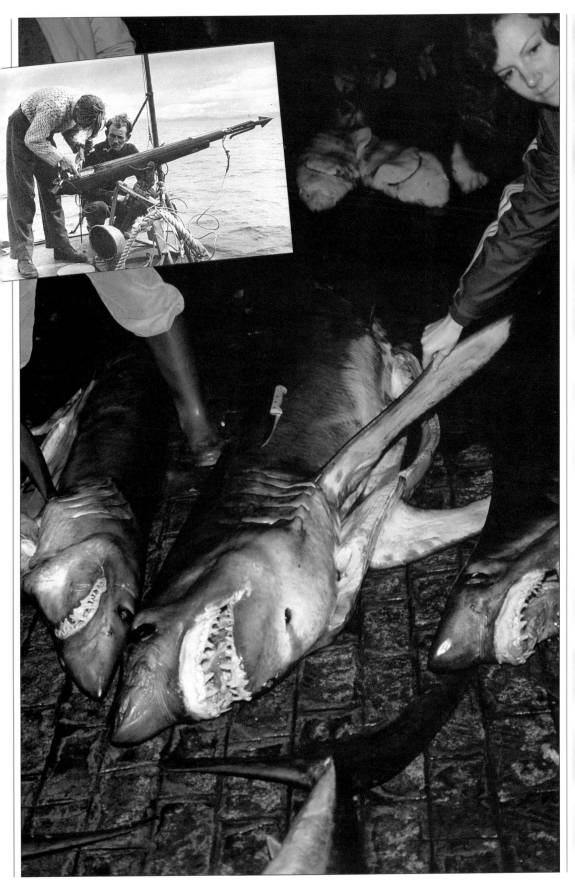

Left ■ A catch of Longfin Mako sharks *Isurus paucus,* a relatively rare species found in tropical Pacific waters. The difficulty for game fishermen is to recognize a rare from a common shark species, before it is gaffed and landed.

Above ■ The Black-tip shark *Carcharhinus limbatus* is a fast-moving fish-eating species which may be dangerous when food is present. They are aggressive enough to go for fishing lures (see here as a yellow plug), and are renowned for their jumping ability in shallow waters. It is to be hoped that the fishing fraternity will prove to be an effective pro-shark lobby in the long run; no sharks, no sport.

That the Basking shark has been grossly over-exploited is undeniable. If there had been no over-fishing, the catch would have remained roughly constant and the yield-to-fishing-effort ratio would have been unchanged. The figures also reveal that the slaughter rate is greater than the *Cetorhinus* reproduction rate, but do not reveal anything about the biology of the fishes. There is no doubt that some protection measures must be taken if this spectacular species is to survive.

First, the number of sharks will fall to such a low level that fishing for them will become uneconomical, and the trade will stop. Whether this will happen before the population becomes too small for it to recover is debatable. The spring shoaling and surface feeding habits militate against it. The ship that finds the last small shoal will reap a rich but final reward.

Second, for political reasons, a quota system limiting the number caught will be introduced. Such quotas are, however, difficult to police effectively and of little use in conservation. A dead shark discarded by a factory because its acceptance would exceed the checkable quota may be a financial disappointment to the boat's crew, but dead sharks do not reproduce. There is already a quota system within EEC waters for catches by Norwegian boats. In 1985 this was 800 metric tons of liver, a figure that was reduced to 400 metric tons in 1986. The imposition of the quota was not for the purpose of conservation but was part of a fishery package deal. Even so, bureaucracy was behind the times – for in both these two years the quota was not reached.

Third, a complete ban on Basking shark catches could be implemented. This would be the ideal situation because (a) it is extremely easy to enforce, (b) it would enable the populations to rebuild their numbers while they can still do so, and (c) it would cause little financial hardship to countries concerned. For example, in 1985 the sharks caught by Norway were worth an amount of money of significance to an individual, but quite insignificant as a proportion of a nation's gross national product (a tiny seven million pounds sterling). The long-term ecological, conservation and financial benefits of a Basking shark fishing moratorium are extremely clear. All that is needed now is for governments to realize that the long-term benefits outweigh the short-term profits – and to act accordingly . . . before there are no Basking sharks. It is important to note, though, that such solutions can only be effective if collective, not just individual, action is taken. All countries must co-operate.

If all countries were to cooperate, shark farming might be a practicable alternative in a manner akin to farming cattle. The fish caught could then be utilized fully and taken only in such numbers as not to diminish the reservoir stocks.

And as an illustration both of the maximum utilization and of inhumanly cruel wastage of those caught, it is instructive to contrast two situations. Take the case of dogfish landed at Grimsby in north-eastern England. At a factory the thick epaxial (back) muscles are removed and sold as rock salmon or huss for human consumption. Shark flesh is a particularly good meat because it is low in cholesterol. The thin hypaxial (flank and belly) muscles are sold to Germany, where they are regarded as a delicacy. The tails go to the Far East as a basis for soup. The cartilage of the fins and spines is dried, ground into a powder and sold in Hong Kong as an 'aphrodisiac'. Most of the rest of the fish is turned into fishmeal. Hardly any is wasted.

Now consider the very different treatment that sharks receive off Florida. In a report dated January 1989 it was stated that more than 50,000 sharks had been caught off Florida in 1988. They were mostly blacktip sharks, shoals of which were located by the spotter planes that directed the fishing boats. In this way most of each shoal can be caught and a single boat can bring in 1,000 sharks in one haul – a profitable venture. However, although the shark meat is palatable and delicious, it does not fetch a high price. The fins do fetch a high price: over 12 times that of the flesh. So the fins are cut off the live sharks, the main bodies of which are then, as waste, thrown back into the sea to avoid the cost of transportation back to port and subsequent disposal. The sharks,

finless but still alive, are left to die slowly of starvation and infection in the sea, out of sight of human sensibilities. Yet it is to sharks that we attribute the quality of cruelty.

This despite the considerable possibility that sharks could be of great benefit to the human race. Antigens in shark serum, for example, have been shown to slow down the spread of some cancers in humans. Experiments on hamsters have revealed that injections of serum from adult sharks have pre-

Below ■ Dr Gruber manhandles a four-foot Black-tip into the holding tank, ready for photographing (see page 90). The shark was caught with a noose.

cluded the development of tumours that should have formed as a result of the injection of adenovirus tumour cells. The well-known and normally harmless bacterium *Escherichia coli*, which can nevertheless sometimes cause diarrhoea, is killed by shark serum. We do not yet know what are the active factors. We do not yet know what other benefits sharks may yield. We may never know if one species of shark has the most effective remedy to human ailments if the species becomes extinct through our own efforts before we find out. If we are not very careful we will never know.

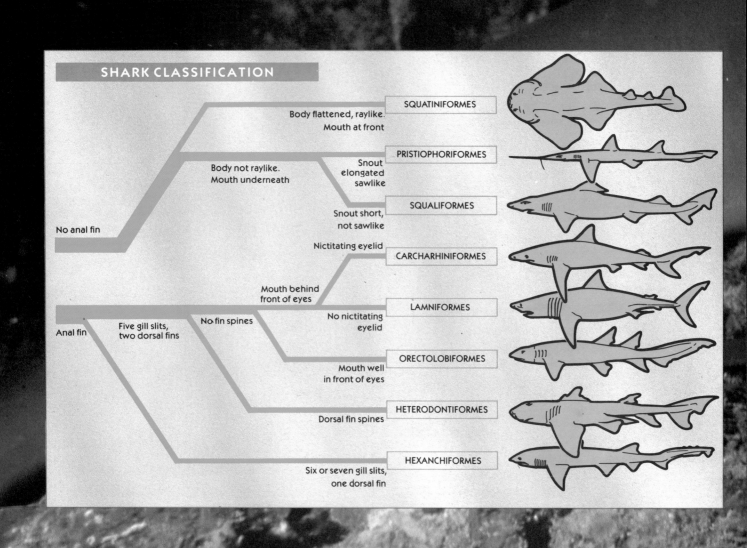

SHARK CLASSIFICATION

No anal fin

Body flattened, raylike. Mouth at front — SQUATINIFORMES

Body not raylike. Mouth underneath

Snout elongated sawlike — PRISTIOPHORIFORMES

Snout short, not sawlike — SQUALIFORMES

Anal fin

Five gill slits, two dorsal fins

No fin spines

Mouth behind front of eyes

Nictitating eyelid — CARCHARHINIFORMES

No nictitating eyelid — LAMNIFORMES

Mouth well in front of eyes — ORECTOLOBIFORMES

Dorsal fin spines — HETERODONTIFORMES

Six or seven gill slits, one dorsal fin — HEXANCHIFORMES

SHARK SPECIES DIRECTORY

For many years it was thought that sharks had to keep swimming to avoid drowning, because the amount of water passing over the gills would be insufficient to maintain respiration. This is not the case: several species have been found 'sleeping', like this White-tip, on the sea bed.

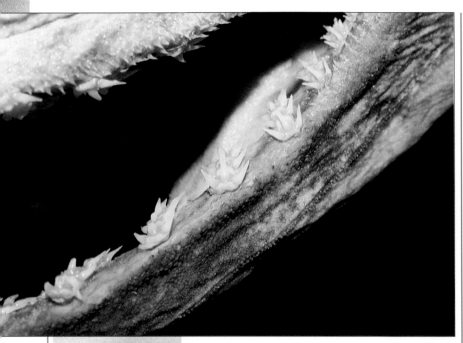

Families are themselves grouped together into orders. Orders' names end in -iformes. Thus the families Scylorhinidae, Triakidae, Sphyrinidae, and Carcharinidae are all families of the order Carcharini-formes. (Neither the family name nor the order name are italicized as the generic and species scientific names are.)

All sharks are classified in any of eight orders.

Second, it is practically impossible to produce a key that enables all sharks to be identified. Many species are distinguished by experts only on the basis of small differences in the ratios of body pro-portions. Even these can change during the growth of an individual fish.

However, in the list below (in which, within orders, the families, genera and species are arranged alpha-betically) diagnostic characters for the higher cate-gories are given where possible. Frequently used, well-known common names are given where pos-sible. Many species have no widely accepted common names or none at all. In some lists, common names based on an anglicization of the scientific name or just invented for that list, are given. They have no validity and are of little use and so are not included below.

Above ■ The small tricuspid (three-pointed) teeth of the Frilled shark *Chlamydoselachus anguineus.*

Right ■ *Chlamydoselachus anguineus* – Frilled shark.

In this section an attempt has been made to list all recognized species of shark. Except by the scienti-fic workers whose classifications have been used for the relevant parts of this list, there will not be universal agreement on all points of the list. There will not be universal agreement about any list so compiled, because there is still much uncertainty over the validity of described species and of the relationships of species as reflected in the classifi-cation. Every shark expert will, however, agree with some – but different – parts of this list.

Some points of explanation are necessary.

First, the scientific names of the species form the basis of this list. This is because the common (non-scientific) names of those sharks that have them vary from country to country. By contrast, the scientific name is universal and governed by a strict code.

Each scientific name is in two parts. For example, consider *Carcharinus leucas*. This widespread spe-cies has many common names – Bull shark, Zambezi shark, Lake Nicaragua shark, Square-nose shark, and many more. The one scientific name applies to all and avoids confusion and misunderstanding. The first part, *Carcharinus*, is the generic name, the second part is the specific or trivial name. Thus *Carcharinus leucas*, *Carcharinus galapagensis*, *Carcharinus melanopterus*, and so on are all different species of the genus *Carcharinus*. Some genera contain many species; some only one.

Genera are in turn grouped together into 'families'. The scientific name of a family ends in -idae. Thus, for example *Carcharinus*, *Negaprion*, *Prionace*, and *Triaenodon* are all genera of the family Carcharinidae.

This order of two families contains shark species with six or more gill slits, only one dorsal fin without spines, and one anal fin.

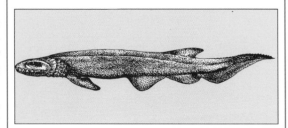

■ FAMILY 1 ■

CHLAMYDOSELACHIDAE 1 genus

Chlamydoselachus – 1 sp.

■ *C. ANGUINEUS* – Frilled shark

Deep, cool ocean waters. Ovoviviparous. Fish eater. Grows to 2m (6½ft).

This elongated, deep-water shark possesses a number of characteristics which clearly resemble those present in early sharks of the palaeozoic era. So striking are these similarities that *Chamydose-lachus* has often been referred to as a 'living fossil'.

However, it is still a matter of controversy whether the Frilled shark is a surviving member of an ancient group of sharks or whether it is a highly derived representative of a living group. To express the dilemma another way, the question remains whether the characteristics are really primitive or have been modified into a pseudoprimitive state from those present in other modern sharks.

These allegedly primitive features include the possession of a notochord (a firm but pliable rod of cartilage that is the precursor of the segmented 'backbone' of other vertebrates) and lateral line grooves that are unroofed for most of their length. In more advanced fishes the notochord has been replaced by articulated segments – the vertebrae – and the lateral line grooves have descended into the skin for protection and only communicate to the exterior by pores adapted for that purpose.

The Frilled shark has six gill slits and each gill slit has a frilled posterior margin. The anterior frill is continuous across the underside of the head, occasioning another common name – the Collar shark.

The teeth have three slender, hooked cusps and resemble the head of a trident. They are not large, but because there are some 300 of them, they provide the Frilled shark with almost a thousand sharp hooks to prevent a prey from escaping.

As might be expected in an animal that spends much of its life in waters into which little light filters, the eyes are large and elongated. Most captures suggest that it lives below 180m (575ft) on the edges of the continental shelves. The largest proportion of specimens have been caught off Japan and some authorities have suggested that for some as yet unknown reason it may live at lesser depths in that region.

The Frilled shark first came to the attention of the scientific world in about 1880. Less than 20 years later a pregnant female was caught and some aspects of the shark's reproductive pattern were discovered. Only one ovary (usually the right) functions at any one time. Eggs are present at all stages of development, and there is no breeding season. There may be up to a dozen mature eggs, each nearly 10cm (4in) across and enclosed in a strong, keratinous egg-shaped case. The young, which have external gills, leave the egg while it is still inside the mother and continue to grow in the uterus until developed enough to be expelled by the mother to lead independent lives.

The diet of the Frilled shark is uncertain – most captures have empty stomachs – but they probably feed on small fish and squid. Certainly, many of those caught on deep-sea lines have taken the squid used as bait.

Chlamydoselachus seems not to be common anywhere. More have been observed in Japanese waters than elsewhere, but others have been caught off New Zealand, Norway and California. It is probably a worldwide species in temperate and subtropical waters.

FAMILY 2
HEXANCHIDAE 3 genera

Heptranchias – 1 sp.

■ *H.PERLO* – Seven-gill shark
Probably worldwide, mostly deep water. Ovoviviparous. Fish eater. Grows to 1.5m (5ft) (females).

This is a slender species with a narrow head and a long, pointed snout. The teeth vary in shape according to their position in the jaws, but all have a large anterior cusp, preceded by a few small cusps and followed by a small series of cusps gradually diminishing in size.

The males are smaller than the female growing, respectively to about 1m (3ft) and about 1.5m (5ft).

It lives in moderately deep warm waters (50–400m, [150–1300ft] rarely to 800m [2,600ft]) at the edge of the continental shelf. Its diet consists largely of fish (especially hake in Atlantic waters) but includes squids and crustaceans. The Seven-gill shark is ovoviviparous; an adult female gives birth to 10 to 20 young, each about 25cm (10in) long.

The distribution of this species is interesting. Although it is probably worldwide in tropical and

Above ■ Hexanchus griseus – Bluntnose six-gilled shark; a highly predatory shark known to feed on seals and large fish.

subtropical waters, only in a few regions is it fairly common. One such region is around the coasts of Spain, where it incurs the displeasure of fishermen by feeding extensively on the commercially important hake.

Hexanchus – 2 spp.

- **H.GRISEUS** – Cow shark or Six-gill shark
- **H.NAKAMURAI** – Bigeyed Six-gill shark

The two species of this genus can be distinguished by the fact that the head is shorter and broader in *H. griseus*, which also has six rows of lateral teeth in the lower jaw, whereas *H. nakamurai*, which favours warmer waters, has a longer, narrower head and five rows of teeth in the lower jaw. The dorsal fin is further forward in the latter species.

The Cow shark is almost worldwide in cooler waters at depths from 100 to 2,000m (325 to 6,500ft) and usually lives close to the bottom. It is a sluggish species, feeding on fishes and crustaceans. A large female grows to about 5m (16ft) long, is ovoviviparous, and may give birth to up to 100 pups, 60–70cm (2ft) long at birth.

The Bigeyed Six-gill shark lives at lesser depths in warmer waters and spends more time away from the seabed, feeding largely on fishes. Also ovoviviparous, a large female may grow to nearly 2m (6½ft) and give birth to more than 20 pups each 40–45cm (1½ft) long.

Notorhynchus – 1 sp.

- **N.CEPEDIANUS** – Seven-gill shark

The Seven-gill shark can reach 4m (13ft) in length. It is widespread, especially in the Indopacific region; in South Australian and Californian waters it is considered dangerous and aggressive. A fish eater, it preys especially on rays and other sharks.

Right ■ *Heterodontus galeatus* – Crested Bullhead shark; the distribution of Bullhead sharks is limited as they tend to stay in local coastal areas.

HETERODONTIFORMES
(Bullhead sharks or Horn sharks)

This order contains eight species in one family. They are blunt-headed, bulky sharks with small bumps over the eyes. They have both biting and crushing teeth – unusual in sharks – two dorsal fins with spines, one anal fin and five gill slits.

FAMILY 1

HETERODONTIDAE 1 genus

Heterodontus – 8 spp.

- **H.FRANCISCI** – Horned shark
Shallow E Pacific waters.
- **H.GALEATUS** – Crested Bullhead shark
Australian waters.
- **H.JAPANICUS** – Japanese Horn shark
NW Pacific.
- **H.MEXICANUS** – Mexican Horn shark
Shallow E and SE Pacific waters.
- **H.PORTUSJACKSONI** – Port Jackson shark
Australian and New Zealand waters.
- **H.QUOYI** – Galapagos Bullhead shark
Central E Pacific.
- **H.RAMALHEIRA** – Mozambique Bullhead shark
W Indian Ocean.
- **H.ZEBRA** – Zebra Bullhead shark
Australasian waters and northwards.

Bullhead sharks are Indopacific species. They are

relatively sluggish fishes living on or very close to the bottom in shallow waters. All are small, the two largest, *H. portusjacksoni* and *H. galeatus*, rarely growing to 1.5m (3ft). Their main food is molluscs which are crushed by the stout molariform teeth. The pointed 'typical' shark-like teeth are found only at the front of the jaws.

Bullhead sharks lay eggs with spiral cases. Females have been seen carrying eggs in their mouth and 'screwing' them into crevices in rocks or corals to anchor them until they hatch.

Heterodontus francisci has the distinction of being one of the very few shark species whose mating has been observed in captivity. This observation made in the Steinhart Aquarium in San Francisco is described on page 34. All the species thrive in captivity.

ORECTOLOBIFORMES
(Carpet sharks, Nurse sharks and Wobbegongs)

Some authorities place the six families included here within the LAMNIFORMES. They are mostly sluggish, bottom-living fishes – apart from the world's largest fish, the Whale shark, which is a sluggish surface dweller. They have two spineless dorsal fins, one anal fin, five gill slits, and two barbels on the underside of the snout; the mouth is well in front of the eyes.

Carpet sharks have gained their common name from the variety of bright colours that spot and stripe the often colourful background hue. Wobbegong is an Australian aboriginal word. The origin of the popular name Nurse shark is in doubt. It may stem from early observations of sharks giving birth and the assumption that, like mammals, they nursed the young. An alternative explanation is that it is a variant of 'hurse' which, along with the still surviving word 'huss', are old names for small sharks generally. Whatever its origin, the name is known to have been in use in English in 1556.

Most orectolobids are sluggish creatures and spend much time motionless on the bottom. The brilliant colours of many species serve as an effective camouflage against the rocks and corals of the tropical reefs. The camouflage is enhanced in some species by the presence of flaps of skin to disguise the outline of their bodies. As befits bottom-living species, all have flattened bodies, to varying extents. Carpet sharks especially spend most of their lives simply lying on the bottom waiting for unsuspecting prey to pass by.

Despite their sluggishness, Carpet sharks have been involved in attacks on humans. In many cases the shark has been so well disguised that it has been trodden on by a paddler. Resenting this uncalled-for treatment, the shark has retaliated by biting the offending leg. Wobbegong teeth are sharp, pointed, and arranged in several rows. The teeth are not large but the jaws are powerful, and the Wobbegong is reluctant to let go of anything it has seized, as the following story illustrates.

In April 1960, off Freemantle, western Australia, a skin diver speared a Wobbegong. In return, the shark seized the diver's arm. The diver tried to force the Wobbegong's jaws apart with his knife – and failed. He then tried to kill the Wobbegong – and failed. A fellow diver came to the rescue and managed to prise the shark off the first diver's arm, who then swam to the boat towing the shark on his spear cord. As he began to climb into the boat, the Wobbegong bit hold of his buttocks – and it was only when both were in the boat that the shark could be killed and the diver released from both the shark's jaws and his embarrassing predicament.

Apart from the Whale shark described below (whose placement with the orectolobids is uncertain), only one species of this order – the Nurse shark, *Ginglymostoma cirratum* – is found outside Indopacific waters.

The Nurse shark is one of the best-known sharks because it is a lazy inshore species that thrives in captivity. Within the Atlantic it is easily identified by the two barbels on the snout, a feature that is present in all orectolobids. Nurse sharks are gregarious

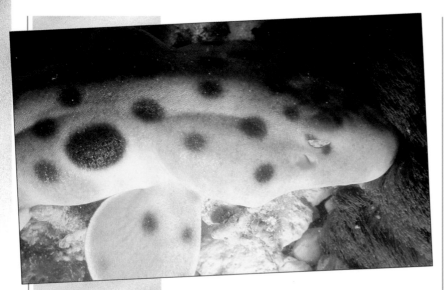

Above ■ Hemiscyllium ocellotum – Epaulette shark; found in shallow Australasian waters.

and frequently rest in groups in water so shallow that their dorsal fins stick out above the surface. Although lazy, they are greedy animals and will take almost any creature that is too slow to get out of the way. Consequently, slow-moving invertebrates and carrion form a large part of their diet.

Experiments carried out in the 1960s showed that Nurse sharks are capable of learning. A young female *Ginglymostoma*, 30cm (1ft) long and weighing about 1kg (2¼lb) was trained to react to one of two targets. The shark pressed the illuminated target and was rewarded with a morsel of food. Within five days the shark achieved 88%, and a few days later it was consistently only just less than 100%, correct. The researchers reported that in this case – with a randomly illuminating target – the shark learned as quickly as a mouse would have.

Because of its availability and docility, the Nurse shark was used in experiments on the efficacy of various shark repellents, along with five other species. Whereas the repellents worked with the other five species, the Nurse shark was completely undeterred by the chemicals.

Reproductive strategy varies within the order. Some species are ovoviviparous, others are egg-layers. For many species the method of reproduction is still unknown and hence is omitted from the list.

FAMILY 1
GINGLYMOSTOMIDAE 2 genera

Ginglymostoma – Nurse sharks 2 spp.

■ ***G.BREVICAUDATUM*** – Nurse shark
Shallow Australian waters. Bottom-feeder. Grows to 75cm (2½ft).

■ ***G.CIRRATUM*** – Nurse shark
Most tropical seas. General bottom-feeder. Grows to about 3m (10ft).

Nebrius – *1 sp.*

■ ***N.FERRUGINEUS*** – Tawny Nurse shark
Widespread, tropical Indopacific. Feeds by suction near the bottom. Nocturnal. Grows to about 3m (10ft).

FAMILY 2
HEMISCYLLIDAE 2 genera

Chiloscyllium – Carpet sharks, Bamboo sharks or Epaulette sharks 9 spp.

■ ***C.ARABICUM*** – Arabian Carpet shark
Bottom-dweller Persian Gulf. Bottom-feeder. Grows to 75cm (2½ft).
■ ***C.BURMENSIS***
N Indian Ocean. Bottom-feeder. Grows to about 50cm (1½ft).
■ ***C.CAERULOPUNCTATUM***
Very poorly known. Off Madagascar. Grows to about 75cm (2½ft).
■ ***C.CONFUSUM***
N Indian Ocean. Diet little known; squid, pieces of shell and an eel have been found in the gut. Grows to about 50cm (1½ft).
■ ***C.GRISEUM*** – Grey Bamboo shark
N Indopacific. Bottom-feeder. Grows to 75cm (2½ft).
■ ***C.HASSELTI***
E Indian waters. Grows to over 50cm (1½ft).
■ ***C.INDICUM***
Australasian waters. Bottom-feeder. Grows to 75cm (2½ft).
■ ***C.PLAGIOSUM***
Australasian waters. Bottom-feeder. Grows to about 1m (3ft).
■ ***C.PUNCTATUM***
Australasian waters. Bottom-feeder. Grows to about 1m (3ft).

Hemiscyllium – Epaulette sharks or Carpet sharks 5 spp.

■ ***H.FREYCINETI***
Shallow Indonesian waters. Bottom-feeder (often in very shallow waters). Grows to about 50cm (1½ft).
■ ***H.HALLSTROMI***
Very poorly known. Indonesian waters. Grows to 75cm (2½ft).

■ *H.OCELLATUM* – Epaulette shark
Australasian waters, often in very shallow waters on reefs. Bottom-feeder. Grows to about 1m (3ft).

■ *H.STRAHANI*
Poorly known. W Pacific. Grows to 75cm (2½ft).

■ *H.TRISPECULARE* – Spectacled Carpet shark
Shallow Australian waters. Bottom-feeder. Grows to 75cm (2½ft).

FAMILY 3

ORECTOLOBIDAE – Wobbegongs 5 genera

Brachaelurus 1 sp.

■ *B.WADDEI* – Blind shark
Australia. Bottom-dweller. Grows to 1.25m (4ft). Known as the Blind shark because it closes its eyelids when out of water.

Eucrossorhinus 1 sp.

■ *E.DASYPOGON* – Tasselled Wobbegong
Australasian waters. Bottom-feeder often in very shallow waters. Grows to over 1m (3ft).

Heteroscyllium 1 sp.

■ *H.COLCLOUGHI*
Only known from Queensland. Grows to 75cm (2½ft).

Orectolobus – Wobbegongs 4 spp.

■ *O.JAPONICUS* – Japanese Wobbegong
W. Pacific, inshore waters. Bottom-feeder. Grows to about 1m (3ft).

■ *O.MACULATUS* – Spotted Wobbegong
W. Pacific and Australia. Bottom-dweller over a wide range of depths. Often partly climbs out of water from one rock pool to another. Feeds on fish and crustaceans attracted by the flaps of skin around the mouth that act as a lure. Grows to over 3m (10ft).

■ *O.ORNATUS* – Carpet shark
W. Pacific and Australia. The common name alludes to its skin pattern. Bottom-feeder. Grows to nearly 3m (10ft).

■ *O.WARDI* – Northern Wobbegong
Australia, shallow warm waters. Bottom-feeder. Grows to about 50cm (1½ft).

Sutorectus 1 sp.

■ *S.TENTACULUS* – Cobbler Wobbegong
Australia, inshore waters. Bottom-feeder. Grows to about 3m (10ft).

FAMILY 4

PARASCYLLIDAE 2 genera

Cirrhoscyllium 3 spp.

■ *C.EXPOLITUM*
Known from only one specimen from the China Sea.

■ *C.FORMOSANUM*
NW Pacific. Bottom-dweller at moderate depth. Grows to 40cm (1½ft).

■ *C.JAPONICUM*
NW Pacific. Bottom-dweller. Grows to 50cm (1½ft).

Parascyllium 4 spp.

■ *P.COLLARE*
SE Australia and Tasmanian waters. Bottom-dweller in fairly deep waters. Grows to over 75cm (2½ft).

■ *P.FERRUGINEUM*
S Australian waters. Bottom-dweller. Grows to about 75cm (2½ft).

■ *P.MULTIMACULATUM* – Tasmanian Carpet shark
Shallow waters around estuaries in Tasmania. Grows to 75cm (2½ft).

■ *P.VARIOLATUM*
Australian waters. Very little known. Eats at least crustaceans. Grows to less than 1m (3ft).

RHINIODONTIDAE 1 genus

Rhiniodon (also, but incorrectly, referred to as *Rhincodon*) 1 sp.

■ *R.TYPUS* – Whale shark
The correct placement of this species is uncertain. The Whale shark is the only species in its family – the Rhiniodontidae. It is also the largest fish in the world. However, it shares two particular attributes with the second largest fish in the world, the Basking shark – to which it is not related. First, both species are inoffensive surface-living filter-feeders, and second, both species have been subject to published exaggerations of their size.

The Whale shark was first brought to the attention of science in April 1828 when a specimen was harpooned in Table Bay, South Africa. The body was seen by an army surgeon, Dr Andrew Smith, who subsequently described and named this giant. That specimen was 4.5m (15ft) long with a circumference of about 3m (10ft). The skin was bought for the then great sum of £6.00 and sent to the Paris Museum. It was later realized that this specimen was of an immature male. For the next 20 years letters from correspondents in outposts of western European empires were appearing in journals relating stories of Whale sharks growing up to 18m (60ft) long.

The next specimen actually available for detailed

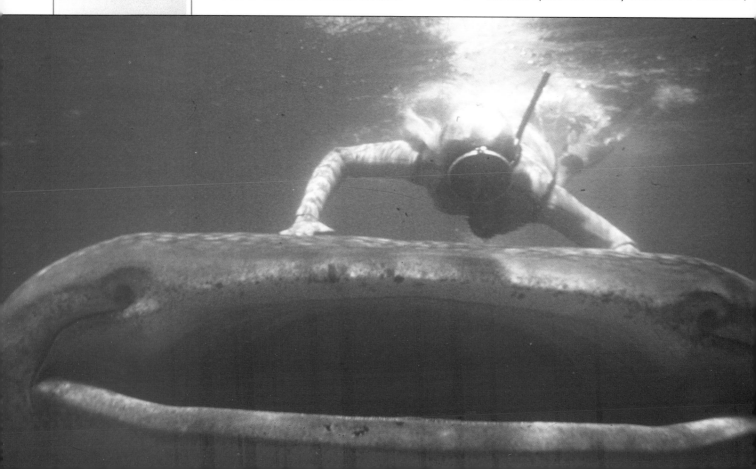

measurement was caught off Ceylon (Sri Lanka) in 1883 and was 7.25m (23½ft) long.

The largest specimen reliably measured came from waters off Florida in 1912. A letter from one of the people involved in the capture, Mr Charles Brooks, of Cleveland, Ohio, sent to Dr Gudger at the American Museum of Natural History, stated that the fish, measured while stranded on a sandbank, was 12m (38ft) long. Later its weight was estimated (unusually, it was probably underestimated) at 5 tons. The estimation of the weight must remain vague. Whatever the weight was, it was great enough to break the timbers when the fish was loaded on to a rail-truck on the slipway.

This specimen was finally stuffed, mounted on a mobile base, and for many years transported around American cities for the delectation of paying audiences. During this phase of its afterlife, it was described as being 14m (45ft) long, and this latter length has often been uncritically quoted in subsequent articles. Some years later when Dr Gudger was able to measure the fish, it had miraculously shrunk to its original 11.7m (38ft) beneath Dr Gudger's magic tape-measure.

Nothing in the above precludes the possibility of Whale sharks of a much greater size. Even in the absence of such monsters, the sizes of parts of a modest Whale shark (10m/32½ft long) are impressive enough. Such a fish would have a tail fin with a vertical span of 4m (13ft), a pectoral fin 2m (6½ft) long, and skin 20cm (8in) thick. From one specimen that was skinned, over half a ton of shavings were pared from the skin before it could be preserved and made supple enough to place over a cast of the body. The mouth was over 1m (4ft) wide. By total contrast, the teeth are minute, barely 2mm (⅒in) long, and arranged in bands along the edge of each jaw.

The Whale shark feeds on plankton and small fish which it sieves from the water as it cruises leisurely around the food-rich surface waters of tropical and subtropical seas. Whereas the sieve of the Basking sharks is formed of erectile gill rakers, that of the Whale shark is formed by a reticulation of tissue, supported by bars of cartilage, between the gill bars. Cruising at only 2–3 knots, thousands of tons of food-containing water are filtered every hour to provide the Whale shark with food. Although the throat has been described as too small to admit any but small food items, there have been rare – and not yet understood – observations of larger fishes 2–3kg (4½–7lb) in weight apparently jumping into the mouth of a Whale shark while it was feeding, vertically aligned, on shoals of smaller fishes.

The lifestyle of the Whale shark pre-empts any notions of aggressiveness. Indeed, it is frequently described as docile and even tolerates scuba divers hitching a ride on its fins. Its lethargic approach to life has led to the demise of scores of individuals who have been inadvertently rammed by ships. By contrast, there is only one recorded instance in which a Whale shark could be assumed to have 'deliberately' attacked a small boat – and even that assumption may be based on a misinterpretation of the fish's activity.

Nothing is known about the longevity of the Whale shark, nor about its seasonal movements, if any. Although its great size and the numerous white spots on the brownish background make it easily identifiable, no consistent observations on an individual have been made. Most sightings are of solitary fish; rarely, small groups have been seen. It is a sad reflection of human ignorance of the world that the total population of the largest of all fishes is unknown.

The species is ovoviviparous: up to 16 eggs have been found inside one female. The young seem to be surprisingly small, 50cm (18 in) long at birth. The earlier, and often repeated, statements that the Whale shark is an egg-layer stem from a most atypical observation made in 1953. In that year, an egg-case was trawled up in the Gulf of Mexico. The egg-case was 30cm (1ft) long, 15cm (6in) broad and 10cm (4in) thick. Inside was an embryo Whale shark about 40cm (18in) long and nearly full term. There was no doubt about its identity – the white spots, broad head, terminal mouth and longitudinal ridges on the back were all present. It was a miniature of the adult. However, this find is the only Whale shark egg found outside the mother. Because it was the first ever found it was assumed that egg-laying was the normal mode of reproduction. All subsequent pregnant female Whale sharks caught have retained the eggs, and it is now evident that it was just bad luck that the first egg found was prematurely ejected from the mother.

Above ∎ The enormity of a Whale shark was appreciated by thousands of Americans when this species went on tour in 1913.

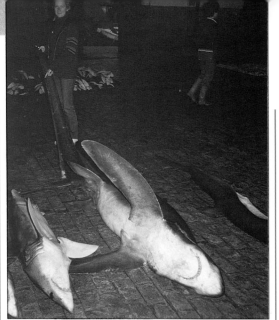

Right ■ A Bigeye Thresher shark *Alopias superciliosus* caught off Atlantic Morocco. The upper lobe of the tail of Threshers can be as long as the body itself.

■ **F A M I L Y 6** ■

STEGOSTOMATIDAE 1 genus

Stegostoma – 1 spp.

■ **S. FASCIATUM** – Zebra shark
Widespread in the Indopacific region. Bottom-dweller in shallow waters. Sluggish, bottom-feeder. Grows to over 3m (10ft). This species is often, and possibly better, placed in the family Orectolobidae.

LAMNIFORMES

The composition of this order and its relationship with the previous order are very uncertain. In the opinion of different experts many of the families listed here are of other orders. Some authorities conversely consider that the orectolobids should all be placed in the Lamniformes. Here, the families included in the Lamniformes lack the nictitating eyelid present in most orectolobids and have an underslung, not terminal, mouth. They have two spineless dorsal fins, an anal fin, and five gill slits, and many species lack gill rakers. The order is here regarded as containing seven families.

■ **F A M I L Y 1** ■

ALOPIIDAE Thresher sharks 1 genus
The common name alludes to the elongated upper lobe of the caudal fin.

Alopias 3 spp.

■ **A. PELAGICUS**
Warm waters, almost worldwide except for the Atlantic. Surface-feeder. Ovoviviparous. Grows to a total length of over 3m (10ft).
■ **A. SUPERCILIOSUS** – Bigeye Thresher
Most tropical and temperate waters. Ovoviviparous. Fish eater. Grows to about 4m (13ft).

■ **A. VULPINUS** – Thresher or Fox shark
Worldwide in temperate or tropical seas. Fish eater. Ovoviviparous. Grows to a total length (including the tail fin) of 5m (16ft).

Several species of sharks, by virtue of their size, alleged ferocity or other form of quirkiness, have attracted general attention, usually inaccurate. The Thresher sharks can be included in this company.

The physical quirkiness of the Threshers is undeniable. Whereas most sharks have the upper lobe of the tail larger than the lower, only the Threshers have the upper lobe as long as the body. This extreme peculiarity has given rise to much speculation about the use to which this elongated appendage could be put. As usual, most of the early observations were misinterpreted and some of these misinterpretations have long been perpetuated. To minimize the chance of clarification even further, there have been very few sightings of free-swimming Thresher sharks by competent observers.

Early reports told of a slapping noise when six Thresher sharks apparently attacked a small school of dolphins. Another report cites an observation of a Thresher striking a wounded seabird (a diver) and then eating the stunned creature. Several works mention birds as an item of Thresher diet – but whether these reports are based on an analysis of stomach contents or stem from the observation (made off Ireland in the 1850s) quoted above is unclear.

In the early part of this century the belief became current that the Thresher herded shoals of small fish into a denser aggregation using its tail, and then went among them to feed. It was doubted that the elongated tail was strong enough to hit the fish but was adequately made for a 'sheep-dog' function.

It was not until July 1923 that a reliable account of Thresher shark feeding habits was available. Then a Thresher was observed chasing a small fish (about 30cm (1ft) long). When close, the Thresher turned and gave what was described as 'a coach-whip lash with the tail' which was immediately repeated with equal speed. The prey fish was badly injured and sank, scarcely able to swim. Only the presence of the observer prevented the shark from getting its food. How common this use of its tail is, and how the shark can use it with such accuracy, is unknown. That the tail is used in feeding is not in doubt; the mystery is just how it is used.

The lack of observations has hampered understanding of the sharks' feeding strategy, even though Thresher sharks are widely distributed. The three species between them occur in most tropical, subtropical and temperate seas. *Alopias pelagicus* is confined to the Pacific. Of the other two species, the common Thresher *A. vulpinus* is the most wide-spread. In the Atlantic it has been recorded in waters north of Britain. This species is the largest of the three and may reach over 5m (16ft) in total length.

All species have small triangular teeth which they use to hold on to moderate-sized prey or to grab and swallow whole small fish. Squids and pelagic crustaceans have also been reported from sharks' stomachs.

There is some evidence that they hunt in loose, small groups. Off the south-eastern USA they are reported to migrate into deeper water in winter.

Little is known of its life history, although there have been statements to the effect that females are not mature until over 3m (10ft) long; males are slightly smaller. The eggs hatch inside the mother (ovovivi-parity) and are released when about 120cm (4ft) long. Only two, three or four are born at one time. During their time in the uterus, the developing young are fed on infertile eggs produced by the mother – a phenomenon called intrauterine oophagy.

Small, sub-adult Thresher sharks are almost un-known to observers, but are highly desired by large aquaria that wish to display and study them. So far, however, none has been captured.

The flesh is tasty and they are a highly prized catch for any fisherman lucky enough to take one.

The two Atlantic species occur together from southern Spain southwards. They can be distin-guished by the much larger eye of *Alopias super-ciliosus* (up to 10cm/4in across), a species that is thought also to favour somewhat deeper water.

■■■■ F A M I L Y 2 ■■■■
CETORHINIDAE – Basking shark 1 genus

Cetorhinus 1 sp.

■ C.MAXIMUS
Worldwide, surface-feeder on plankton. Apparently hibernates in winter when plankton is scarce. The world's second largest fish.

The English common name alludes to its often-seen habit of basking at the surface of the sea. While basking, the first dorsal fin and the tip of the tail stick out of the water and the fish moves very slowly. The real reason for this behaviour is uncertain, but two suggestions – one more probable than the other – have been proposed. The more likely is that the shark swims slowly because the plankton, on which it feeds, is very densely concentrated at that point.

Less likely is the possibility that this behaviour may be correlated with breeding behaviour.

DISTRIBUTION
The Basking shark is a fish of temperate waters occurring in most coastal regions except at the poles and the equator. It lives off both coasts of the north Pacific, off southern Australia and New Zealand, and around South Africa. It extends about as far north as Ecuador on the Pacific coast of South America, where the Humboldt current brings cold Antarctic water almost up to the equator. By contrast – and to emphasize the importance of water temperature on distribution – it is found only to about the level of São Paulo on the Atlantic coast of South America, where the cold waters of the west wind drift are prevented from going northwards by the South Atlantic equatorial current. In the North Atlantic, the Basking shark rarely straggles south of Cape Cod on the American side, and is found northwards to Ice-

Below ■ *Alopias vulpinus* – Thresher shark, caught off Long Island, New York; besides fish, Threshers are known to take squid, octopus and crustaceans.

Basking sharks filter planktonic food out of the water using comb-like gill rakers which line their gills. The rakers are lost during the winter when feeding ceases.

land past northern Norway to the Barents Sea, around the coasts of Great Britain and north-west Europe, to the western part of the Mediterranean, and south to about the level of the Canary Islands.

The patchy distribution of this species – the great distance separating the northern hemisphere and southern hemisphere populations, and the gaps between the populations in each hemisphere – has given weight to the argument that there may be more than one species of Basking shark. At the moment all specimens are regarded as belonging to *Cetorhinus maximus*, the only species in the genus. However, further research may show that there are more than one species. Observations have been made that suggest that Australian specimens consistently differ in certain bodily proportions from those of the North Atlantic.

COLOUR

The Basking shark is greyish-brown to slaty grey, or almost black, dorsally. The underside may be a uniform paler variety of the colour on top, or grade into an off-white. Sometimes there is a triangular white patch beneath the snout. A variable, although uncommon, feature is the presence of two pale or white bands along either side of the ventral midline.

SIZE

The Basking shark is the second largest fish in the world, and certainly the largest regularly appearing in European waters. In suggesting a maximum size, most books usually quote a phrase such as 13m (40ft) or more', which is probably something (yet again) of an exaggeration. As far as research can discover, the longest specimen actually cited as measured was 11m (36ft) long, but other data (such as where, when and by whom) are lacking. The largest specimen ever sold to a fishery firm in Monterey, California, was 'a few inches less than 30 feet'. It therefore seems likely that the Basking shark rarely grows to more than 10m (30ft) in length. The Basking shark is still an impressive fish: the Monterey specimen mentioned above weighed 3,900kg (8,600lb) or almost four tons. By contrast, the smallest free-living specimen caught was measured as 165cm (5ft 5in) long.

GENERAL BIOLOGY

The Basking shark is one of the most easily recognizable sharks, and not just because of its size. It has a bluntly pointed snout which in a large specimen extends about 45cm (18in) in front of the mouth. Smaller specimens have a more sharply pointed snout. Particularly characteristic are the very long gill slits which almost meet their partners at the dorsal

and ventral mid-lines. These allow the huge amounts of water sieved in feeding to flow back to the sea.

Basking sharks feed by filtering plankton out of the water. Plankton consists of minute floating organisms, both plant and animal. It includes the larval forms of fishes, crustaceans and other invertebrates whose life is dictated by the direction of the water currents and the temperature. As the water warms up in spring and early summer, so the number of organisms increases rapidly. In the winter the plankton population is sparse – so sparse, in fact, that a Basking shark would use up more energy in swimming around filtering out its food than it would gain from the calorific value of the food. Basking sharks therefore do not feed in winter; instead they undergo a sort of hibernation in deep water.

The plankton is filtered out by a mesh of gill rakers, which are fine, bristle-like structures borne on the gill arches. There are over a thousand on each side of each gill slit. The rakers are slightly flexible and each has mucus-secreting glands at the base. Muscles attached here erect the rakers as the shark opens its mouth to form the sieve between the slits. As the mouth is closed and the water is squeezed out, the plankton is entangled in the mucus, the rakers lie flat on the surface of each arch and the food is squeezed into the mouth. The gill rakers are lost during winter when feeding ceases.

A reasonably large Basking shark 7m (23ft) long, when feeding, swims at about 2km/1¼ miles per hour, and with a gill area of 270m² (325 sq. yd) filters about 1,500m³ per hour (about a third of a million gallons of water per hour). The teeth are minute (about 3mm/⅛in high) and are not used in feeding.

The Basking sharks' seasonal migrations have long been observed – they move inshore in spring and early summer – but the movements are variable and unpredictable. A controlling factor over their appearance at the surface, and over where they appear, is the availability of food. It has been found that off the Newfoundland coast they are rarely seen if the water temperature is below 6°C (43°F), and that they are most numerous when the surface water is between 8 and 13°C/46–55°F (when the plankton concentration is at its highest).

The large stomach may contain over half a ton of plankton, which itself is about 30% organic matter. Opening up the stomach of a Basking shark produces an avalanche of nutritious red mulch. The red colour comes from the pigment present especially in planktonic crustaceans. The digested food is stored as oil (squalene) in the fish's liver – a large organ that can weigh up to 25% of the total weight of the fish.

The large, oil-rich liver acts to some extent as a hydrostatic organ (oil is lighter than water), but even so, overall the shark is denser than water and sinks when dead. The oil has also been the cause of the slaughter of Basking shark populations in recent years as the fish have been hunted for this commercially desirable commodity.

The migrations, both in direction and purpose, have long been a source of scientific controversy. There is no doubt that feeding is a major motive, as has been described. In feeding, groups or individuals cruise leisurely, and seemingly at random, at the surface. Breeding has never been observed, but there are a few observations of surface behaviour that may have some bearing upon breeding. Basking sharks have sometimes been seen swimming close together in pairs. Off the European coasts there have been sightings of various numbers swimming nose to tail in variously-sized circles. It is possible that either of these activities may be some form of courtship, but copulation has never been seen. The ratio of the number of females to males varies from 40:1 to 18:1, based on capture records of fisheries. Whether this means that there are more females than males, or whether females are more often at the surface, and hence caught, is unknown.

As with most sharks, very little is known about the method of reproduction of this species. Only once has a birth been seen, and that was when a harpooned female was being towed ashore and ejected five living and one dead offspring. The young were about 1.5m (5ft) long and lacked any umbilical cord. It seems therefore that the smaller free-living Basking sharks caught – the smallest was 165cm (5ft 5in) – are the young of the year. It is known from dissections of dead specimens that only the right ovary is functional. This contains about 6 million yolky eggs that ripen when about 1cm (¼in) in diameter. Most of them degenerate. Females that bear signs of having copulated recently have been caught, but no pregnant females (except the one mentioned above) are known. It is probable that with the onset of pregnancy the females move off the coasts and into deeper water, a behaviour pattern not unknown in other shark species.

How often they breed, how long the gestation period is and how many viable young are produced is unknown. If the Basking shark follows trends seen in other large sharks, then they probably produce 2 to 4 young at a time. The life expectancy is unknown, but if the slow reproduction rate is correctly surmised they may well live for some 30 years.

FAMILY 3
LAMNIDAE 3 genera

Carcharodon – 1 sp.

■ *C. CARCHARIAS* – Great White shark

DISTRIBUTION

Sometimes alternatively called white death, the Man-eater, the White Pointer (in Australia) or the Blue Pointer (in South Africa), the shark is found, now in decreasing numbers, in all tropical, subtropical and temperate seas. It is most often recorded in relatively shallow offshore waters. It may well occur in deeper waters but has not been noticed there. It appears to prefer subtropical waters to temperate waters. The Great White shark has been recorded within the Mediterranean Sea, and there are reliable records of its occurrence around the coasts of Britain up to about the middle of the last century, especially around the Cornish peninsula and in the Bristol Channel. Whether as a result of climatic changes, pollution, or lack of food (probably a combination of all three factors), none has been seen this century in British coastal waters.

COLOUR

Despite the common names (and this is an example of a fault in many common names), the Great White shark is not white. A large specimen is slaty grey, dun, blue, or very dark grey on the back and top of the sides. This darker colour changes abruptly to a cream or dirty white to pale grey on the lower part of the sides and belly. There is a black spot in the 'armpit' of each pectoral fin and these fins are often dark-tipped. The eyes are black.

SIZE

Although the Great White is the largest of the carnivorous sharks, it does not reach the size alleged in

Left ■ The characteristic protruding snout and long gill slits of the Basking shark.

Above ■ The last few feet of an attacking lunge are made blind by the Great White shark, as the eyes roll back to provide extra protection.

popular literature and in the films. The largest accurately measured specimen, caught off Cuba in 1945, was 6.4m (21ft) long and weighed 3,312kg (7,302lb) or over 3 tons. Of moderate reliability is an unsubstantiated report of a specimen 9m (29ft) long caught off the Azores in 1978. In a slightly less reliable category still is the report of an 11.3m/37ft-long fish from New Brunswick, Canada, in the 1930s. Perhaps more interesting (and revealing because it indicates our lack of knowledge of this species) is that small specimens are practically unknown.

In many books, fossil and sub-fossil teeth belonging to a fish called *Carcharodon megalodon* have been cited as proving that recently extinct relatives of the Great White shark were up to 30m (100ft) long. These teeth, very similar to those of the extant Great White but about twice the size (up to 12cm/4½in long and about the same measurement across the blade) have been found on the floor of the North

Atlantic and South Pacific and in recent deposits in Europe, New Zealand, East Asia, Africa, South America and the eastern USA. From these teeth, enthusiasts have extrapolated that their original owners were almost 30m (100ft) long. Indeed, in 1909 the American Museum of Natural History reconstructed a jaw of *C. megalodon*, basing it on the dimensions of the living Great White, and produced a jaw with a breadth of 2.75m (9ft) and a gape of nearly 2m (6½ft). From this jaw a fish of 24m (78ft) in length was predicated.

However, such reasoning is flawed. Although there is no doubt that *C. megalodon* teeth are more than twice the size of *C. carcharias* teeth, there is no evidence that the same number of teeth adorned the jaws. Recently, it has been suggested that *C. megalodon* had relatively few teeth. Dating these teeth has not been easy, but from the thickness of the manganese dioxide deposit on one from the

South Pacific it has been calculated that it was separated from its owner just over 11,000 years ago. Only finding a complete fossilized specimen or a complete set of jaws (both extremely unlikely events) will solve this puzzle.

GENERAL BIOLOGY

Very little is known about the biology of the Great White shark. It is not evenly distributed throughout its range, nor necessarily throughout the year at any one locality. There is some slight evidence that this species may show some territoriality, returning to the same coastal area year after year. At least some sharks appear in the same region each year, although as yet there is only one observation that the same individuals are involved. There was one large female fish, recognized by a characteristic scar, which repeatedly returned to the same area of South Australia annually for 13 years. A puzzling amendment to this observation as published was that this female appeared not to have increased in size during this period. In that the fish was weighed neither at the start nor at the end of this period, such a statement is impossible to substantiate. Nonetheless, without qualification, it appears in books.

Certainly, there is some seasonality. Based on angling records, it seems that most big-game specimens are caught in South Australian waters in January, and fewer between September to April. In Victorian waters, April and July are the most productive months; in Queensland, May and June.

Should such a seasonal migration to and from recognized coastal sites be affirmed as a common phenomenon in this species, where they go when not around the coast is not known. It has been suggested that the offshore movements may be for breeding. One fish tagged in shallow water was observed six months later only 1km (½ mile) away from the tagging site. This strengthens the idea that they may not move far from their chosen coastal resort.

There seems, in some areas to be a grouping of Great White sharks according to age and sex, factors in shoal determination reasonably common in sharks. For example, around one reef off Australia, the average Great White shark observed at one time was male and from 3 to 5m (10 to 16ft) long. Some miles to the west of that reef, most observed there were female and from 5 to 6m (16 to 19½ft) long.

Juvenile Great White sharks are hardly ever caught. A recent account cited about 160cm (5ft) as the length of the smallest specimens. There is an often, but uncritically, quoted report of a pregnant female being caught at Agamy, near Alexandria, in the Mediterranean in 1934. This fish was 4.5m (14ft) long

and weighed about 2.5 tons. Subsequent butchering revealed the presence of 9 young, each about 66cm (2ft) long and weighing 49kg (108lb). This report is suspect. First there is no certainty that the species was correctly identified. Second, the total weight of the embryos is nearly half a ton, which is a suspiciously high proportion of the mother's weight. Third, a 160cm/5ft-long free-swimming Great White shark weighs only 20–25kg (50–60lb). Recent guesses have suggested that the young of the Great White are about 1m (3ft) long at birth, and that the mother reaches sexual maturity at about 3.5 to 4.5m (11 to 14ft) in length. The age of the mother at sexual maturity is unknown, as is the life expectancy of the species, although ages of respectively 10 years and 40–50 years have been suggested. Neither the mating, nor pupping areas are known. The relative frequency of small specimens in one part of the western North Atlantic has led to postulations that the waters off Montauk Point, Long Island may be a pupping region. If, as is likely, the reproduction of the Great White shark is like that of other lamnid sharks, it will give birth to a few, well-formed young, possibly only every alternate year.

The Great White shark swims with a stiff-bodied motion; although the body is relatively flexible, the deep anterior part precludes the sinuosity of movement present in shallower-bodied sharks. The heat generated by muscular activity raises the internal temperature of the Great White to a level higher than in the surrounding water. One fish about 4m (13ft) long, which had been kept immobile for three hours and so had cooled down, still had a body temperature 2°C (4°F) above that of the sea.

Having a body temperature higher than that of the sea is beneficial to the shark because it enables the biological processes to function more efficiently. To this end, the Great White has developed a counter-current heat-exchange system between its blood-vessels to minimize heat loss. This heat-exchange system relies on the fact that arteries which run from the inside of the body to the surface lie alongside veins which run back to the inside. Thus, as the warm blood flows along each artery, it transfers heat to the cooler blood running from the skin to the inside of the fish in the vein. This warms up the venous blood, so minimizing chilling at the centre of the shark. In this way, the Great White may be able to keep its body up to 10°C (18°F) higher than the surrounding water. There is, however, one drawback to this otherwise beneficial system – there is the risk that the shark could overheat in very warm weather. This risk is reflected in the fact that the Great White is scarce in tropical waters and much favours the cooler subtropical and temperate waters.

The Great White has keen senses of smell and vision. Indeed, its vision is thought to be important in its hunting. An odd observation is that the sharks raise their heads out of the water, allegedly to see better. If that is indeed the reason for this action, certain important points are raised. The refractive index for water is different from that of air, and fish eyes are naturally adapted for seeing under water, not in air. The only fish that has eyes adapted to see in both media – the four-eyed fish, *Anableps* – has each lens horizontally divided into two parts: the upper part has a surface curvature for vision in air, the lower part has a curvature adapted for vision in water. How the Great White shark copes with vision in the two media (if it does cope with it at all) is unknown.

The main food items of the Great White shark are seals and sea lions, although fish are also taken. Their reputation as man-eaters is unjustified. They hardly ever eat human flesh. From below, a man swimming looks a bit like a sea mammal (the shark's usual food) and may be mistaken for one. Once the shark has tasted the flesh, however, the victim is usually rejected because a person has the wrong taste. Nonetheless, the injuries caused to the swimmer may prove fatal, especially if a vital artery is severed.

Like all other sharks, the Great White has an electro-receptive sense. It is thought that some attacks on small boats are the result of the shark's being attracted by the electric field set up between the metal of the boat and the sea water and so mistaking the boat for a prey item.

Although the Great White shark is a predator, it does not spend all its time hunting fearlessly. Indeed, its behaviour is very variable and quite unpredictable. It does not always attack a suitable prey item. Sometimes it just investigates, presumably out of a sort of shark-type curiosity. There have even been reports of the Great White exhibiting behaviour which, anthropomorphically, has been interpreted as cowardice. One such report comes from Jacques Cousteau, one of the pioneer underwater explorers and photographers. He describes an encounter with an 8m (25ft) Great White shark which was swimming lazily only 13m (40ft) away from Cousteau and a companion off the Cape Verde Islands. Cousteau wrote: 'Then the shark saw us. His reaction was the least conceivable one. In pure fright, the monster voided a cloud of excrement and departed at an incredible speed.'

Despite the fact that humans are not a favoured item on the Great White's menu, the Great White's flesh is regarded highly by many people. Just after

World War I R. J. Coles wrote that its flesh was 'the most delicious [he] had ever tasted'. Whereas most sharks have pale flesh with a low oil content, the Great White has reddish flesh (like that of salmon in colour) and is fat, soft and appetizing.

Isurus 2 or 3 spp.

The isurids are known colloquially as Mackerel sharks. One species, *Isurus oxyrinchus*, is commonly called the Mako; this name is not a corruption of 'mackerel' but a Maori word for shark that has passed into our language. (Actually, the Maoris use the same word 'Mako' for a small tree with bright red flowers.)

Mackerel sharks are elegant, slender creatures with conical, pointed snouts. They are a popular game fish, and not just because their flesh is tasty and succulent. Once hooked, a Mackerel shark puts up a prodigious fight and makes spectacular leaps in trying to free itself.

There are either two or three species. The uncertainty arises because the Indian Ocean species (*Isurus alatus*) is believed by some authorities to be the same species as the widespread long-finned Mako, *Isurus paucus*. It may well be some time before this taxonomic puzzle is solved because it is known that fin shape and relative size varies with the growth of these fishes. For example, in *Isurus oxyrinchus*, the dorsal fin is short and rounded in juveniles but becomes tall and sharply pointed in adults. At all stages they swim at the surface with the dorsal fin exposed, so the shape of the dorsal fin assumed an unwarranted importance as a diagnostic characteristic. Until the change of shape of the dorsal fin with maturation was appreciated, different stages in the life of *Isurus oxyrinchus* were considered to be, and were described as, different species.

The Mako is a solitary fish for most of its life and feeds on other pelagic fast-swimming fishes such as tuna. Not surprisingly, therefore, the Mako is one of the swiftest of fishes and has been measured at swimming speeds of 100km per hour (60mph).

Characteristic of Makos (to distinguish them from the closely related porbeagles) is the presence of only one lateral keel on the tail and the lack of lateral cusps on the teeth. The lobes of the caudal fin form a more acute angle than they do in Porbeagles.

In the Long-fin Mako, the pectoral fins are about as long as the head, whereas in the Mako they are only about two-thirds of the head's length. Both species are blue above (a deep blue in the case of the Mako and a more intense blue in the Long-fin Mako) and white ventrally. The transition between the two colours is abrupt.

Both the Mako and the Long-fin Mako are cosmopolitan in temperate and tropical seas. The Mako reaches 3m (10ft) in length, about a metre less than the Long-fin Mako. The former species is more tolerant of cooler waters and has been caught off northwestern Scotland. The Long-fin Mako prefers warmer seas, but even there its distribution is patchy.

Little is known of the Mako's life. Both species are ovoviviparous. Neither species is prolific: the Mako has only a few young at a time, and they are 60–70cm (2ft) long at birth. The young of the Long-fin Mako are larger (around 90cm (3ft) at birth) and usually there are only two. The Long-fin Mako males mature at just under 2.5m (8ft) and the females at just over. The lifespan is unknown.

Mako weighing up to 450kg (1,000lb) have been caught on rod and line. Even around British coasts, rod-caught Mako up to 170kg (400lb) have been recorded.

■ *I.ALATUS*
A rare species from the Indian Ocean. Characterized by long pectoral fins it is not recognized as an independent species by all authorities.

■ *I.OXYRINCHUS* – Mako
Widespread in all warm seas. Fish eater. Ovoviviparous. Grows to well over 3m (10ft).

■ *I.PAUCUS* – Long-fin Mako
Widespread, but patchy, in deeper warm and temperate seas.
Ovoviviparous. Grows to about 4m (13ft).

Lamna 2 spp.

■ *L.DITROPIS* – Pacific Porbeagle
Temperate waters of N Pacific. Fish eater. Ovoviviparous. Grows to about 3m (10ft).

■ *L.NASUS* – Porbeagle
Cold and temperate waters, but almost worldwide. Fish eater. Ovoviviparous. Grows to about 3m (10ft).

The Porbeagle (*Lamna nasus*) is closely related to the Mako shark but can be distinguished by its stockier, more powerful body and by the presence of a second lateral keel below the midline lateral keel. The teeth have two small basal cusps that are not present in the Mako shark.

The common name 'Porbeagle' is a hybrid of 'porpoise' and 'beagle' coined (or at least first printed) by William Borlase in 1758. At one stage during the last century the Porbeagle was also known as the Beaumaris shark, which was thought to be a different species, and is found as such in Victorian natural histories.

The Porbeagle occurs around coasts but is also oceanic. It favours midwaters and is commonest around 200–700m (650–2,275ft) in depth. In the North Atlantic it extends well beyond the arctic circle. In some areas it is common. Formerly, it was sufficiently common off Scandinavia for it to be the subject of a thriving Norwegian fishery. The Norwegians exported the flesh particularly to Italy, where it had a ready market as a delicacy. However, the fishery did not survive the rate of exploitation put upon it. Once common in the area, Porbeagle numbers fell sharply.

Fishes with such slow replacement rates grow slowly and/or have few young. Next to nothing is known about the growth rate of the Porbeagle. They do have only few young (less than 4) but these are large – some 75cm (2ft) long at birth, weighing nearly 10kg (20lb). In that Porbeagles have not become extinct, it should be possible – with sufficient caution in the exploitation of existing stocks – to find out the growth rate.

Unusually, the males tend to be larger than the females. An adult male averages 2.6m (8ft 6in) long, and adult female only 2.2m (7ft 2in). Specimens over 3.5m (11½ft) long have been reliably reported.

Throughout most of its range, it seems that the Porbeagle undergoes a seasonal migration, living closer to the shore in summer and migrating to the deeper, warmer waters in winter. The Porbeagle is not, however, present in the North Pacific. There, its place is taken by its close relative, *Lamna ditropis*.

Like its relative the Mako, the fast-swimming Porbeagle often has a body temperature higher than that of the surrounding water. Porbeagles swim almost ceaselessly, and the dark red muscle tissue they use for this purpose lies deep in the body, close to the spine. These muscles work more efficiently at a higher temperature so they are located deep down to minimize the loss of heat generated by the muscular activity. The blood supply vessels are modified to ensure an ample supply of oxygen to the dark red muscle while reducing the supply to areas where the blood would cool quickly to no great advantage to the fish. Consequently the muscle temperature is constantly 6–7°C (11–13°F) higher than that of the surrounding water. This characteristic doubtless enables the Porbeagle (and other isurid sharks) to capitalize on the rich pickings in cool waters.

FAMILY 4

MEGACHASMIDAE 1 genus

Megachasma 1 sp.

■ *M.PELAGIOS* – Megamouth

There have been two particularly exciting events in the world of ichthyology during this century. The first was the discovery in 1938 of the coelacanth, a large primitive fish thought to have disappeared along with the dinosaurs over 60 million years ago. The second event was the discovery of a large shark,

popularly (and aptly) called Megamouth, in 1976. In that year, an underwater sea-anchor was taken up from about 200m of water in the Pacific off Hawaii. Entangled in the sea-anchor was a 4.46m- (14½ft-) long shark. A few years later this species was given the scientific name *Megachasma pelagios*, the generic name alluding to the very large mouth and the specific name referring to its pelagic filter-feeding habit. The surprise caused by this discovery was not so much that such a large, moderately deep-water filter-feeding shark should exist at all than that it should have remained hidden in an area where the fish fauna was believed to be well known. A few

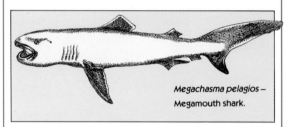

Megachasma pelagios – Megamouth shark.

years later a second, smaller specimen was caught between Hawaii and California. To date, these are the only two specimens properly recorded.

During September 1988, however, a third specimen was reportedly washed up on a beach at Mea Mandurah, a holiday resort south of Perth, Western Australia. This specimen was 4m (13ft) long and had a mouth 80cm (2½ft) across. The report stated that a local fisherman, Zlate Trifunkofski, with the help of others, tried to push the specimen back into the sea. Luckily for shark researchers, this attempt failed.

Why three specimens of this large animal should suddenly have come to light only in the last 12 years is a mystery.

So far, little is known about Megamouth. It has been placed in a family of its own – Megachasmidae – which is probably more closely related to the family Lamnidae (containing the Great White shark) than to the two monotypic families containing the other filter-feeding sharks – the Cetorhinidae (Basking shark) and the Rhiniodontidae (Whale shark). Megamouth feeds on plankton, jellyfish and small squids sieved from deeper waters.

Although plankton are less abundant in twilight zones than at the surface, there are denser layers at certain depths. There, the plankton are sufficiently concentrated to scatter depth-measuring sonar pulses, with the result that they have been called the deep scattering layer. This layer undergoes a daily vertical migration, rising nearer the surface at night and descending by day. It is highly likely that Megamouth lives in the deep scattering layer and follows its daily migration.

The capacious mouth has many small luminous organs and it is believed that the light coming from them may attract the plankton to the shark, rather than merely enable the shark to see the plankton. Small luminous organs are dispersed on the body, but their function is a mystery. The teeth are small, over a hundred rows forming a rasp-like surface to the jaws. The body is very dark brown with hardly any countershading.

FAMILY 5
MITSUKURIDAE 1 genus

Mitsukurina – 1 sp.

■ *M. OWSTONI* – Goblin shark
The most remarkable feature of this shark is the snout, which is greatly elongated and flat and extends well in front of the mouth. Its function is unknown. Beneath the shelf-like snout is the mouth, which has widely protrusible jaws and awl-like teeth. The eye is minute. The body is flabby and light or pinkish grey in colour. The fins and the gill region are darker.

The Goblin shark can attain a length of over 3m (10ft). It is a benthic (bottom-dwelling) species on outer continental slopes from 100 to 700m (325 to 2,275ft) in depth. Its food is mostly benthic invertebrates and small fishes. The flabby body and overall

shape suggest an inactive lifestyle. It is a widespread species – nowhere is it common, but there have been more recoveries off Japan than elsewhere. Whether this reflects a greater number of individuals there or a greater intensity of deep-sea fishing is uncertain. Its mode of reproduction is uncertain but usually presumed to be ovoviviparity.

Fossil sharks' teeth seemingly identical to those of the Goblin shark are known ffrom the Cretaceous deposits of the Middle East. These teeth are assigned to a genus *Scapanorhynchus*, and the attribution of the generic names *Scapanorhynchus* and *Mitsukurina* to the living form has been somewhat haphazard.

Mitsukurina owstoni – Goblin shark.

FAMILY 6
ODONTASPIDAE 2 genera

Eugomphodus – 2 spp.

■ *E. TAURUS* – Sand shark or Sand Tiger shark
Widespread in the Atlantic, W Pacific and around Australia, close to bottom usually at depths less than 70m (230ft). Feeds on fishes, squids and crustaceans. Ovoviviparous. May grow to over 3m (10ft).
■ *E. TRICUSPIDATUS* – Indian Ocean. Very similar to *E. taurus*.

Odontaspis – 2 spp.

■ *O. FEROX* – Small-tooth Sand Tiger
Possibly cosmopolitan, from shallow waters to 400m (1,300ft) depth. Feeds on fishes, squids and crustaceans. Probably ovoviviparous. Grows to over 3m (10ft).
■ *O. NORONHAI* – Known only from deep water off Madeira. Grows to 1.75m (5½ft).

The Sand or Sand Tiger sharks (or, in the case of *Eugomphodus taurus*, the Grey Nurse shark to the Australians) are represented by the two genera listed above. They can be distinguished by the fact the first upper tooth is about the same size as the second in *Eugomphodus* whereas it is much smaller than the second in *Odontaspis*. This distinguishing feature is best verified on dead specimens!

Eugomphodus taurus (often still referred to as *Odontaspis taurus*) is one of the best-known sharks because it is common, widespread, lives in shallow water, and is frequently kept in aquaria.

The Sand Tiger shark *Eugomphodus taurus* has often been blamed for attacks on humans in the United States and Australia, though there has yet to be a verified attack.

The Sand shark occurs in shallow seas and bays (mostly less than 70m/230ft depth) in all subtropical and tropical areas except the eastern Pacific. It is an abundant species – in one summer almost 2,000 were caught over a sandbank off the north-east American coast. There are also reliable reports of schools of 'a couple of hundred' Sand sharks acting in a seemingly co-ordinated way by surrounding and condensing a large shoal of smaller prey fish, chasing them into shallow water, and finally eating the then easily obtainable prey. In some areas Sand sharks wreck fishermen's nets, usually when they are heavy with their catch. Fish (including smaller sharks) are the main item on the Sand shark's menu. Bottom-living invertebrates are also eaten if the effort involved in their seizure is not too great for the shark.

One interesting observation is that in captivity, despite their almost constant swimming, they eat much less than they do in the wild. Some have lived for over 10 years in captivity, and one specimen

seasonal migration, moving offshore to warmer waters when the temperature reaches about 20°C (68°F).

The Sand Tiger shark is ovoviviparous and usually gives birth to just two young, sometimes only one. The reproduction of this species has been studied in some detail (a rare possibility for sharks); even more remarkably, in the course of this study a research scientist was bitten by an unborn pup.

As is relatively usual, only the right ovary is functional, and produces spherical eggs about the size of a garden pea. A small number of eggs – usually less than a couple of dozen – pass into the shell glands (where the thin shell is formed on them) and then into the oviducts where they are fertilized. Under normal circumstances, only one egg in each oviduct hatches and the pup then starts to eat the nearby eggs. To feed the two pups (one in each oviduct) the female continues to produce eggs that remain unfertilized. The pups continue to eat them, and the pups continue to grow until each is about 70cm (2½ft) long (maybe almost one-third of the mother's length). For most of this time in the oviduct – normally about a year – the pups swim around freely and eat avidly. Indeed, the embryo that bit the researcher was only about 25cm (8in) long. Just before birth, the young turn round in the uterus so that their heads face the mother's tail. This makes for an easier birth for both the mother and the young. The mother is then not rasped by the pup's denticles, and the pup's fins do not get caught in the mother. At the time of birth, the stomach of each pup can contain some 700gm (1½lb) of yolk, which, calculating from the small size of each egg and the length of time that the young have been nourished in this way, means that hundreds of thousands of infertile eggs have been produced just to feed the resulting twins.

After birth, the young are left to their own devices. Neither the age of sexual maturity, nor the lifespan of the Sand shark is known.

Not much is known about the life in nature of Sand sharks. They tend to form loose shoals of equal-sized animals. It has been suggested that this is a protective mechanism to prevent larger individuals from eating smaller individuals of the same species.

The Sand shark is sandy in colour, light greyish brown on the back and paler below. Although sometimes not very conspicuous, there are many small, rounded yellow-brown or yellow-ochre spots.

Although still common, the Sand shark is not as common as it once was. Once it was so abundant off Australia that it was caught for the high-grade oil in its liver, which was used as lamp oil particularly

about 3.5m (11½ft) long did so for that period subsisting on some 140kg (300lb) of fish a year. In some months as little as 3kg (6½lb) was eaten.

There is some uncertainty over whether or not they attack humans. They have an unsubstantiated reputation for doing so in parts of Australia and South Africa, yet they have no such reputation in other areas where they are equally common.

In regions where the water undergoes a seasonal change of temperature, Sand sharks undertake a to illuminate dwellings in Sydney in the last century. Now the shark is scarce, or even absent, in some areas around the Australian coast. The reasons for this are not hard to find. It has a slow rate of reproduction and, although no longer caught for its oil, it has suffered heavily at the hands of skindivers. As a shallow-water species, with a suitably impressive set of teeth, it is avidly hunted by divers with spearguns for no motive other than to boost the divers' reputations in the bar later that day.

Above ■ The Bignose shark, *Carcharhinus altimus*, is a typical example of the 'classic' shape of the Requiem sharks.

■ FAMILY 7 ■
PSEUDOCARCHARIIDAE 1 genus

Pseudocarcharias – 1 sp.

■ *P.KAMOHARAI* – Crocodile shark
Inhabitant of open oceans. Slender hook-like teeth. Very few specimens have been caught and little is known about it. Quite why it should have acquired a common name is a mystery. Some authors place this family in the Odontaspidae.

CARCHARINIFORMES

This is the most speciose order of sharks: its 8 families contain more than 200 species – more than half of the known total of extant shark species. Many of the species are difficult to distinguish from each other and look superficially like the archetypal stereotyped concept of a shark.

These sharks have one anal fin, two spineless dorsal fins, and five gill slits, as do the lamniform sharks, but they differ from the members of that order in that usually a nictitating membrane (the 'third' eyelid) is present on the eye. Carcharinids are elegant, sinuous swimmers with hydrodynamically efficient bodies. The snout is pointed and slightly flattened – in the Hammerhead sharks extremely flattened and greatly widened – and the caudal peduncle mostly unkeeled. They are mostly greyish in colour, often with a metallic sheen. In many species the fins have dark or pale tips, but this feature is not present in all species and, when present, is usually less discernible in larger specimens.

The teeth have long, often serrated, cutting edges. They are aligned in two rows along the jaws. The jaw muscles are powerful: carcharinid sharks can easily remove chunks of flesh or amputate limbs. In the latter case especially, the resultant haemorrhaging and shock may prove fatal to humans. Carcharinids have been accused of involvement in attacks on humans, but it is difficult to be certain about which species are involved because many are so similar to an eye that is inexperienced in distinguishing them or affected by the stress of the attack. More easily identified species, such as the Tiger shark, have been positively identified in attacks on humans.

The brains are large, especially in the carcharinid and sphrynid sharks. 'Large' in this case is relative to the brain size in, say, the squalid sharks.

At least in the carcharinid and sphrynids a placenta is developed for the nutrition of the embryos. Male carcharinids have an expansible clasper, a cartilaginous part of which prevents the male from separating from the female during copulation. The reproductive strategy varies. There are ovoviviparous and viviparous species, the latter being the commoner among those species in which the mode of reproduction is known. The female of some of the larger genera (eg *Scoliodon*, *Prionace* and *Carcharinus*) stores sperm in the shell gland until the following spring when she ovulates and the egg is fertilized in the shell gland in the uterus. In genera with a yolk sac placenta gestation can take up to a year, at the end of which about a dozen young may be born. Some species have much larger litters; up to 80 pups have been noted from a large female. Growth rate is uncertain and doubtless very variable among different members of the order, but an increase in length of 40% in the first year has been reported for some carcharinids. It is thought that smaller species may become sexually mature in only a very few years. Lifespan and speed of maturation of larger species is unknown.

Carchariniformes are widespread in all seas and a few species enter freshwater (eg *Carcharinus leucas*). Fish, squids and crustaceans are the main foods.

FAMILY 1
CARCHARINIDAE 12 genera

Carcharinus – .c.90 spp.

This genus of about 90 species is usually known as Requiem sharks, although particular species have their own, often locally variable, common names. The origin of the adjective 'requiem' is uncertain. One theory is that it derives from the French word for shark – *requin*. Another theory is that the word originates from 'rest', as reputedly used in *The History of the Caribbean Islands* published in 1666. There it is written that 'the shark fish is known as the requiem . . . that is to say, rest, haply because he is wont to appear in fair weather.'

In view of the general similarity of many of the species, only a few for which there is sufficient information have here been singled out for more detailed treatment as representatives of their genus.

■ *C.ACRONOTUS* – Blacknose shark
Atlantic Ocean. Grows to 2m (6½ft).

■ *C.ALBIMARGINATUS* – Silvertip shark
Widespread in Indopacific. Grows to 3m (10ft).

■ *C.ALTIMUS*
Deep waters of Atlantic and Indopacific. Grows to 3m (10ft).

■ *C.AMBLYRHYNCHOIDES*
W. Pacific and Australia. Grows to 1.75m (5½ft).

■ *C.AMBLYRHYNCHS* – Grey Reef shark

W Pacific and Indian Oceans, Australia. Common in lagoons and around reefs. Grows to 2.5m (8ft).
This is a frequently photographed species because it is common around reefs and in shallow waters and is sufficiently shark-like to impress those to whom the photographs are subsequently shown. The Grey Reef shark seems to show what could be interpreted as a well-developed curiosity towards anything unusual. It seems not to be an aggressive species, although it has been accused of one attack on humans, but perhaps it was goaded beyond its normal level of tolerance by an interfering and persistent underwater photographer. The Grey Reef shark adopts what is thought to be a threat posture (as do some other carcharinid species) by bending its body and lowering its tail and pectoral fins.

This is one of the few sharks in which a neoplasm (a cancer) has been reported. One specimen so affected was caught at Eniwetok Atoll in 1972. Twenty years before, Eniwetok Atoll had been the site of atomic bomb tests, so perhaps the locality of that survey on shark health was chosen for reasons additional to ordinary marine biology.

Left ■ The Silvertip shark, *Carcharhinus albimarginatus*; this shark is most likely to be found on the seaward side of reefs in the Indo-Pacific, with adults typically inhabiting waters below 25m (80ft).

The Grey Reef shark is an unremarkable species, little known despite being often seen and photographed.

■ *C.AMBOINENSIS*
Indopacific and Australia. Grows to nearly 3m (10ft).

■ *C.BORNEENSIS*
W Pacific. Poorly known. Grows to 75cm (2½ft).

■ *C.BRACHYURUS* – New Zealand whaler
S Indopacific, South Atlantic. Grows to 3m (10ft).

■ *C.BREVIPINNA* – Spinner shark
Most warm seas. Grows to 3m (10ft). The common name alludes to its habit when hooked of leaping from the sea and spinning on its own axis.

■ *C.CAUTUS*
W Pacific and Australia. Grows to 1.5m (5ft).

■ *C.DUSSUMIERI*
N Indian Ocean and W Pacific. Grows to 1m (3ft).

■ *C.FALCIFORMIS* – Silky shark
Widespread except in colder northern waters, the Silky shark is one of the commonest open-ocean sharks. It grows to 3.5m (11½ft). Although the scientific name refers to its sickle-shaped fins, the common name refers to its smooth skin. The denticles are much smaller and flatter than is normal for sharks in general.

There is some evidence that adults in coastal areas may be territorial. Like *Carcharinus amblyrhynchus* it has a threat posture: the back arched, the snout raised and the pectorals lowered, followed by an exaggerated rolling motion. This is most frequently seen when the shark is cornered with no means of escape against a reef by the approach of a larger shark or divers. It has not been proved to have been involved in attacks on humans – but a few slashes may result if its warning display is ignored.

In the Caribbean and the Gulf of Mexico, the pregnant females repair to deeper water (about 100m/325ft) to give birth, so reducing the threat of predation to their pups.

■ *C.FITZRYOENSIS*
Australia. Grows to 1.5m (5ft).

■ *C.GALAPAGENSIS* – Galapagos shark, Grey Reef whaler

Below ■ *Carcharhinus brachyurus* goes by several common names: in New Zealand it is known as the New Zealand Whaler, in Australia as the Bronze Whaler, in the United States as the Narrowtooth shark, and elsewhere as the Copper shark. It grows to a maximum length of about 2.3m (7ft 6in).

The specific name of this species alludes to its occurrence in the waters around the Galapagos Islands in the Pacific Ocean. It is common in the eastern Pacific but may be much more widespread. Species of the genus *Carcharinus* are difficult to distinguish and it is highly probable that there have been mistaken identifications in the past which, if as is likely the body has not been preserved, can never be rectified. The inclusion of a species name in the literature is regrettably not therefore a guarantee of that species' presence in the area under question. A good example of this problem is shown in the case of the Galapagos shark. The first record of *Carcharinus galapagensis* in the Atlantic stemmed from a shark attack on 20 April, 1963 at St Thomas in the Virgin Islands. On that day a US naval officer, John Gibson, was attacked by a shark that bit through his femoral artery and removed parts of his body including his right hand. He died. Lines were set to catch sharks in the Magen's Bay area. The following day a 3m (10ft) shark was caught, and in its stomach were what were alleged to be bits of Mr Gibson's flesh and his right hand. The shark was later identified as *Carcharinus galapagensis*. Whether this identification was correct is unknown and what effect it had on other sharks being so named from both coasts of the tropical Atlantic is also unknown. Currently, how-

Left ■ Grey Reef sharks *Carcharhinus amblyrynchos* are restricted to the Indo-Pacific. In observations of their social behaviour, male Grey Reef sharks have been adjudged to be moving along odour trails produced by females.

Left ■ Despite its common name, the Galapagos shark *Carcharhinus galapagensis* is found in both the Pacific and Atlantic Oceans.

ever, this species is listed as common, especially in the eastern Pacific, and found also in the western Pacific and on both equatorial Atlantic coasts. It has not been reported from the Australasian region.

The Galapagos shark is charcoal grey above and white to pale grey below. The species has been reported growing to about 3.7m (12ft) long, but is mostly somewhat smaller. The females are usually larger than the males, averaging about 2.7m (9ft) to the males' 2.3m (7½ft).

Tagging experiments on this species have given researchers some idea of shark growth rates. Two individuals of 1.14m (3¼ft) and 1.4m (4½ft) were tagged. Just over five years later they were recaptured with the respective lengths of 1.4m (4½ft) and 1.58m (5ft). Although the smaller individual had grown faster than the larger (260mm/10in as against 180mm/7in), its growth rate was still slow: only 50mm (2in) per year.

This species is abundant in parts of its range, and juveniles especially are aggressive and/or curious. Interpretations placed on their behaviour doubtless reflect the degree of fear the observer has of sharks.

The juveniles (1–2m/3–6½ft) tend to follow and bump into small boats, oars, pieces of submerged equipment, divers, or anything else that seemingly takes their interest.

An expedition in 1956 noted large numbers of young Galapagos sharks 'patrolling' a reef flat, often in water so shallow that their backs were unprotected from the tropical sun. These sharks 'joined in' the expedition's fish-collecting activities and were unaffected by rotenone – the poison used to collect reef-dwelling and secretive fishes. The Galapagos sharks indulged in feeding frenzies when high explosive was used to stun fishes for collecting purposes.

Yet some months later, an expedition member made the following observations. 'The larger Galapagos sharks were sometimes followed by schools of starry jacks (*Caranx stellatus*) or groups of rainbow runners (*Elegatis bipinnulatus*) which continually scratched themselves on the obviously irritated sharks. On one occasion, a large rainbow runner bumped into a small shark causing it to disgorge some food which the more agile runner promptly

The Bull shark, *Carcharhinus leucas,* will feed in fresh and salt water; how it overcomes the lethal problem of osmotic exchange is unknown.

swallowed. These fish would often leave their host to take bits of food or swirl around fish too large for them to eat. The action seemed to attract the attention of the shark, which would move in and feed.'

■ C. HEMIODON
East Indies, Australia. Grows to 1.75m (5½ft).

■ C. ISODON
W Atlantic. Grows to almost 2m (6½ft).

■ C. LEUCAS – Bull shark

This is a widespread species, found in all shallow tropical and temperate seas. It is not found in the coldest seas and is scarce in the north-east Atlantic. Biologically, it is one of the most unusual sharks in that it frequently enters rivers and lakes. The selection of previously quoted common names reflects this tendency, but the Zambezi shark and the Lake Nicaragua shark are now known to be (probably transient) populations of the Bull shark. It has even been found in the Upper Amazon, some 3,000km (1,875 miles) from the sea. Elsewhere it has been found in the Mississippi River, rivers in Guatemala, and in the Limpopo River. At this last locality, where it is not uncommon at some times of the year, it has been known to attack a hippopotamus, thereby making *Carcharinus leucas* the only shark likely to have included the 'river horse' in its menu. It is very likely to have attacked humans in freshwater but because crocodiles and alligators occur in the same regions there may well have been confusion over the originator of the attack. In some freshwaters – such as Lake Nicaragua and its outflow, the Río San Juan – it is common enough to be caught for food.

Although the Bull shark feeds in both fresh and salt water, it breeds only in the sea. Off East Africa, for example, five or six young some 60cm (2ft) long are delivered in shallow waters. There appears to be no care for the young; in fact, the converse may be true, for there are many reports of the Bull shark eagerly eating its own young, certainly the offspring of the species if not the offspring of the individual observed.

Off the southern African coast, Bull sharks are most numerous in estuaries between December and March. During this time, the Zambezi, Limpopo and other rivers are in flood and the sharks congregate in the estuaries to scavenge on the food brought down by the rivers. It is also during this period, when the shallow seas are warm and muddy, that most attacks on humans have taken place. Shark nets have proved an effective deterrent in these areas, but for the nets to be effective people must swim between them and the shore. One who swam outside the net was Mr P. Sithole at Margate, Natal, on Christmas Eve, 1960. He was seen to have been partly thrust out of the water, 'screaming and flailing'. He then disappeared silently. Later, his corpse was washed ashore. His left leg was completely missing, as was the right leg below the knee. This attack was attributed to a Bull shark – although how that species was positively identified as the attacker remains a mystery.

The Bull shark grows to about 3m (10ft) long, is grey in colour, lighter underneath, and the juveniles have dark tips to their fins. It is otherwise indistinctive and very likely to be confused with other shallow-water carcharinids It is unselective in its diet (hippo notwithstanding). What is remarkable about the Bull shark, though, is not just that it regularly goes into freshwater but that it is the only shark that does so so often.

Unless the concentration of salts in the body fluids of fishes is the same as that of the surrounding water, fish have a problem with osmosis – the relative flow of water and dissolved salts between the tissues and the surrounding medium in an attempt to balance the internal and external concentration. This is a physical phenomenon which has to be surmounted by biological factors for the animals to survive. If a marine fish, for example, took no biological remedial action, it would lose its body water to the sea, become dehydrated and died – because sea water is more concentrated than its own fluids. Sharks (a marine group) overcome this problem by retaining urea in their body fluids to balance the fluids' concentration with that of sea water, so that the threat of dehydration by osmosis is reduced. While this system has evolved in and works satisfactorily for sharks spending all their lives in the sea, the reverse problem is presented to a shark entering fresh water. In fresh water, the shark's body fluids are now more concentrated than the surrounding medium. Theoretically, the shark should swell, its tissues become waterlogged and burst, and it should die. This is why most sharks do not go far into fresh water; they soon feel unwell. If they stayed they would die, so they retreat to stay alive. How the Bull shark overcomes this problem is not known with certainty. A number of species of bony fishes either seasonally or irregularly change from a sea to a fresh water environment, and something is known of their physiological defence mechanisms against the effects of osmosis. Why, of all the sharks, only one species has developed such an anti-osmotic defence mechanism is unknown.

■ C. LIMBATUS – Black-tip shark
Cosmopolitan in shallow seas. To 2.25m (7½ft).

■ C. LONGIMANUS – Oceanic White-tip shark. To 4m (13ft).

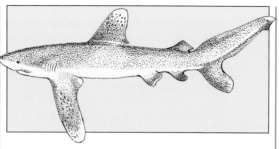

This is a cosmopolitan open-ocean species of all warm and temperate seas, although it has not been recorded with any degree of certainty in the Mediterranean. It is rarely encountered around the shoreline but is reputed to congregate around ship-wrecks to scavenge on carrion. It is commonest where water temperature is over 21°C (70°F) and more than 200m (650ft) deep.

It is bronze-grey dorsally, paler ventrally, the characteristically rounded tip of the first dorsal white. The tips of the pectoral fins and the tip of the lower lobe of the caudal are usually white.

They give birth in the early summer to 6–9 pups up to 75cm (2½ft) long. Birth occurs in nursery grounds near the equator. The growth of the young is rapid, and they may reach sexual maturity in as little as two years. They grow to 4m (13ft) long.

Oceanic whitetips feed on fish, squid and swimming crabs. They are usually described as sluggish swimmers, but can make short, fast spurts. It was once thought that their top speed was considerable because tuna – among the fastest of all fishes – had been found in their stomachs. One observation on the Oceanic White-tip's feeding, however, suggests that guile, not speed, might be the reason for the inclusion of nutritious tuna in their diet. A school of tuna, each about 7kg (15½lb) in weight, were feeding on their prey fish, making their characteristic short, fast rushes and often leaping out of the water. Swimming among this shoal of tuna was a group of Oceanic White-tips, moving lazily about 3m (10ft) apart and following an irregular sinuous course. The sharks did not appear to pursue the tuna but just swam about with their mouths wide open and their snouts protruding above the surface. The conclusion reached was that the sharks were simply waiting for tuna to swim or leap into their mouths during the feeding excitement. And because most sharks are not renowned for their speed, the conclusion from that observation does seem to fit in with general shark lifestyle.

■ *C.MACLOTI*
N and W Indopacific. Grows to 1m (3ft).

■ *C.MELANOPTERUS* – Black-tip Reef shark, Whaler, or Black-tip shark

This species has a dark tip to the first dorsal fin, anal fin and lower lobe of the caudal fin. The other fins may also have darkened tips. It is common and territorial around reefs, and may often be found in water shallow enough for the first dorsal fin to clear the surface of the water.

Its reputation varies with the authority. Some authors call it aggressive; others state that it backs off when confronted. A possible cause of these irreconcilable opinions is the difficulty of distinguishing *C. melanopterus* from the similar, also black-tipped, *C. limbatus*, or even *C. leucas* and *C. falciformis*. To the untrained eye, specific determination of many species of *Carcharinus* is impossible.

Carcharinus melanopterus gives birth in shallow water to between four and 14 pups each about 50cm (1½ft) long. Larger females give birth to a greater number of young. The gestation period is 12–16 months. Although the sharks mature at about 1.1m (3½ft), the length of time it takes for them to reach sexual maturity is unknown, as is the lifespan. A large adult can grow to 1.8m (6ft) in length.

The distribution of this species is interesting and may well have been changed by human activity. It is widespread in the south-western Pacific, in eastern and western parts of the Indian Ocean, and in the Red Sea. In the Mediterranean it is common only in the south-eastern part from Israel round to Tunisia. This Mediterranean distribution and the absence of any records from there during the 19th century suggests that it has moved into that basin from the Red Sea via the Suez Canal. As it continues to spread westward towards the Atlantic (which it has not yet reached), it would certainly seem that the construction of the Suez Canal is allowing at least this species of shark to increase its range and distribution from the Indopacific to the Atlantic Oceans.

■ *C.OBSCURUS* – Dusky shark
Cosmopolitan except for colder waters. Grows to 4m (13ft).

Above ■ Looking like some kind of elegant space ship, a Sandbar shark cruises out of the blackness. This sluggish, bottom-dwelling shark is often eaten by its close cousin, the Bull shark.

Left ■ A Black-tip Reef shark *Carcharhinus melanopterus*, also known as a Whaler shark; in common with other fish species, sharks tend to be white on the undersides so that when seen from below, they blend with the lighter background of the sky.

Right ■ The Sandbar shark is viviparous, producing a litter of up to 14 pups every two to three years.

■ *C.PEREZI* – Caribbean Reef shark
W Atlantic and Caribbean. Common in the West Indies around reefs. Grows to 3m (10ft).

■ *C.PLUMBEUS* – Sandbar shark
This rather stocky, heavy-bodied species is found in most tropical and temperate seas except the eastern Pacific. It is a bottom-dweller from estuaries down to the edge of the continental shelf. It rarely ventures into fresh water. Although found over all substrates, it prefers sandy bottoms to muddy bottoms. It is a sandy grey to bronze above, paler ventrally. The undersides of the pectoral fins may have dark tips.

The Sandbar shark is a viviparous species, giving birth to one litter every 2–3 years, up to 14 young some 50cm (1½ft) long being born in shallow water. The gestation period is about a year. They become sexually mature at about 1.75m (5½ft) long, and can reach 2.5m (8ft) long.

There is an anomaly in the sex ratio of this species. In most species the number of males to females is about 1:1; in the Sandbar shark there are five females to each male. More puzzling from the point of view of the success of the species are the facts that a large proportion of the females are not gravid and, furthermore, only one oviduct seems to be functional. It is not known whether the unusual sex ratio and poor fecundity of the females is the result of some inherent mating difficulties or whether the numbers of males has been reduced because fewer reach maturity due to excess predation or some other factor affecting their viability.

The Sandbar shark is possibly closely related to the Bull shark, for the Sandbar shark also frequents estuaries. If they are related, there is no show of fraternal affection, for the Sandbar shark is extensively eaten by the Bull shark. Perhaps just because it is sluggish, the Sandbar shark features in other sharks' diets. Two whole Sandbar sharks each 2m (6½ft) long, were found in the stomach of a Great White shark, itself only 5m (16ft) long.

■ *C.POROSUS*
SE Pacific and S Atlantic. Lives close to the bottom; may enter estuaries. Grows to 1.5m (5ft).

■ *C.SEALEI*
Australasia. Grows to 1m (3ft).

■ *C.SIGNATUS*
Atlantic. Lives at depths by day; migrates to surface at night. Grows to nearly 3m (10ft). Has green eyes when alive.

■ *C.SORRAH*
Indopacific to Australasia. Common around reefs. Grows to over 1.5m (5ft).

■ *C.WHEELERI*
Indian Ocean. Grows to 1.75m (5½ft).

Galeocerdo – 1 sp.

■ *G.CUVIERI* – Tiger shark

This distinctive species is reputed to be second only to the Great White shark in the league table of attacks on humans. In this one case it is possible to be fairly certain that the species was correctly identified because the Tiger shark is sufficiently distinctive for there to be little chance of confusion with other species.

It has a flattened head and a body that is stout in the pectoral region but tapers evenly to a shallow caudal peduncle which, unusually for a carcharinid, has a lateral keel. The body is greenish-grey to brown above, and paler ventrally. In the juveniles there are vertical rows of conspicuous dark spots which merge in the adults to form the vertical dark bars that give the tiger shark its common name. The stripes begin to fade in sharks of more than 3m (10ft) in length. It commonly grows to 4m (13ft) long, and some individuals may grow to over 6m (19½ft).

It is a widespread species, usually found close to coasts and near the bottom. Although most common in tropical seas, one has been recorded from eastern Iceland. It is a powerful but most leisurely swimmer and has been seen apparently sunning itself at the surface. It is an omnivorous species, eating sea birds, crustaceans, fish, turtles, sea mammals, molluscs and garbage. The teeth are large, serrated, and have a distinctive shape.

Little is known of its life. It is ovoviviparous and after a gestation period of possibly 16 months, the female gives birth to a large litter. Forty young are not uncommon and up to 80 pups have been recorded. Despite the large litters, the Tiger shark is not abundant anywhere. The absence of detailed knowledge of the relative density of shark populations precludes comment on what has been described as a 'substantial *Galeocerdo* population'. In December 1958 the son of a restaurateur in Oahu, a Mr Weaver, was killed by a Tiger shark while playing on an airbed off the east coast of that island. This

Left ■ The Tiger shark *Galeocerdo cuvier* is easily recognized by the stripes along its flanks.

incident stimulated the local population into massacring sharks in some pointless attempt at revenge. The result was that more than 500 sharks were killed, of which 71 were Tiger sharks. This does seem a high proportion but there is no information on the area of search, nor the degree of selective killings of that distinctive species.

There is one observation that may shed an unusual light on Tiger shark behaviour. In one area of the Gulf of Mexico sharks, including several medium-sized Tiger sharks, were found lying in underwater caves, seemingly asleep. At least, the sharks were lying on the floor of the cave immobile apart from gentle movements of their gills. They had their mouths open and did not react to the presence of the divers. Continued investigation of this phenomenon showed that the water in the cave was less saline than the surrounding sea as fresh water emerged from underground springs into the sea cave. It was suggested that this less salty water had a slightly narcotic effect on the sharks which they 'enjoy'. It was further suggested that sharks may search out such secluded and safe areas for some form of communal shark relaxation. Whatever the true explanation of this phenomenon may be (if the offered explanation is not right), the suggestion pleasantly redresses some of the antisocial activities attributed to sharks.

Left ■ The distribution of the Blackspot shark *Carcharhinus sealei* is restricted to the Indo-Pacific region.

Overleaf ■ The magnificent Tiger shark, cruising in the Bahamas.

Glyphis – 2 spp.

■ **G.GANGETICUS** – Ganges shark
N Indian Ocean. Very frequently in fresh water, common in estuaries. Grows to over 2m (6½ft).
■ **G.GLYPHIS**
Poorly known. Recorded from Indonesia and N Australia. Grows possibly to 3m (10ft).

Isogomphodon – 1 sp.

■ **I.OXYRHYNCHUS**
SW Atlantic. Inshore and estuarine waters. Grows to 1.5m (5ft).

Lamniopsis – 1 sp.

■ **L.TEMMINCKI**
N Indian Ocean and Indonesia. Shallow waters. Grows to 1.75m (5½ft).

Loxodon – 1 sp.

■ **L.MACRORHINUS**
Indian Ocean. Grows to less than 1m (3ft).

Nasolamia – 1 sp.

■ **N.VELOX**
E and SE Pacific. Poorly known. Grows to 1.5m (5ft).

Negaprion – Lemon sharks 2 spp.

Despite some recent statements to the contrary, only two species are now included in this genus. However, the peculiar distribution of these two species has caused some difficulty in reconciling the specimens recorded with the species identified. It is possible that the specific determination of some specimens may well be changed to produce a more coherent range for the comprising species.

The Lemon sharks are sluggish fishes tolerant of many conditions including high water temperatures (30°C/86°F) and low oxygen concentration. They are therefore commonly kept in captivity, both for public display and for scientific research. A large proportion of scientific knowledge of shark physiology comes from this species. In other chapters in this book some of the generalizations about shark physiology are based on findings derived from Lemon sharks.

Lemon sharks are heavily built, sluggish animals spending much time being sedentary if ample food is available. They derive their common name from their colour, which is yellowish brown to yellow ochre above, paling to lemon yellow or dirty white ventrally. They are found close inshore and, as an example of the tolerance that has led to their desirability as aquarium exhibits can even tolerate a short stay in fresh waters (although their ability so to do is minimal compared with that of the bull shark).

Usually inhabitants of shallow water, they are rarely found at depth. The small eyes are ill adapted for vision in low light areas.

They are viviparous. The females give birth to up to 15 young, some 60cm (2ft) long, in shallow protected waters; lagoons are favoured. Research off the Atlantic coast of North America reveals that they tend to stay within a small nursery area of less than 10km^2 (4 square miles) of shallow water. They gradually extend their range until they become mature, when they may undertake long migrations. They are probably about seven years old at sexual maturity. Adults tend to form loose shoals of a couple of dozen individuals, the shoals segregated by sex. Mating occurs (in the areas studied) in spring or early summer, and gestation lasts up to 14 months depending upon the temperature.

They eat almost anything that lives close to the bottom or fails to evade their jaws. Lemon sharks are more active at night than during the day.

In some areas Lemon sharks form the basis of a fishery in which their skins are used for leather, their fins for soup, and their muscles as high-quality fish flesh, while their liver oil is extracted for its high Vitamin A content.

■ **N.ACUTIDENS** – Sicklefin Lemon shark
W Pacific and Indian Ocean. Coastal waters. Grows to more than 3m (10ft).

■ **N.BREVIROSTRIS** – Lemon shark
E Pacific and temperate Atlantic. Coastal waters. Grows to over 3m (10ft).

Prionace – 1 sp.

■ **P.GLAUCA** – Blue shark
This species is a strong contender for the title of the world's most widespread shark; it has been recorded at many localities from north of Norway to south of Australia. The Australian Blue shark was formerly thought to be a separate species but is not now so regarded.

The Blue shark is a slender, elegant species with a longish pointed snout. The back is bright indigo blue (hence its common name), the belly paler.

The Blue shark female has a thick skin on her back. This secondary sexual characteristic is necessary to prevent her from being damaged by the male's teeth as he bites her on the back to gain a purchase in order to push one of his claspers into her cloaca. Mating occurs in summer and, as in some other carcharinids, the female stores the sperm until she ovulates the following spring. About a year after the egg is fertilized the young are born. Blue shark litters are large; up to 100 pups may be born to a large

female. The pups are about 40cm (16in) long at birth, which usually takes place in the open ocean.

In the northern part of its range, the Blue shark makes a northward and coastal migration in summer. The larger the seasonal surge of Atlantic water, the further north the sharks are found. During the summer there is an extensive sport fishery for this species, especially around the south-west of England and the west of Ireland. An interesting fact is that most of the fishes in these areas are spent or immature females – few males make this migration, staying further out at sea and further south. In the open ocean Blue sharks have often followed boats, presumably to feed on any garbage. Their normal diet consists of pelagic fishes, but there are reports of their eating whale flesh and catching birds.

Although the species may grow to over 3m (10ft) in length, only relatively small specimens form the basis of the lucrative seasonal sport fishing industry off the English Channel. The largest Blue shark caught on rod and line during the summer of 1988 was a 73.5kg (162lb) specimen from Looe, Cornwall.

Rhizoprionodon – 7 spp.

■ **R.ACUTUS**
SE Atlantic and Indopacific. Grows to 1.5m (5ft).

■ **R.LALANDII**
SW Atlantic and Caribbean. Grows to 75cm (2½ft).

■ **R.LONGURIO**
E Pacific. Shallow coastal warm waters. Grows to 1.25m (4ft).

■ **R.OLOGOLINX**
NE Indian Ocean. Grows to 70cm (2½ft).

■ **R.POROSUS**
SW Atlantic and Caribbean. Common in a wide range of depths. May enter estuaries. Grows to 1.25m (4ft).

■ **R.TAYLORI**
Australia. Grows to 75cm (2½ft).

■ **R.TERRAENOVAE**
NW Atlantic and Caribbean. Common in shallow waters and estuaries. Grows to over 1m (3ft).

Scoliodon – 1 sp.

■ **S.LATICAUDUS**
N Indian Ocean. Shallow waters and estuaries. Grows to 75cm (2½ft).

Triaenodon – 1 sp.

■ **T.OBESUS** – White-tip Reef shark
This shark is widespread throughout the Indopacific

Right ■ The Blue shark *Prionace glauca* is a wide-ranging open ocean and coastal species, found from surface waters to depths of 150m.

region. It is particularly common around reefs and like other reef sharks it is much photographed. It is a sluggish species, largely nocturnal in habit and in some areas passes the day sleeping in caves to avoid the aquatic paparazzi. Although widespread and easily seen, little is known of its life. It feeds on fish and invertebrates, grows to over 2m (6½ft) long and, unless speared or otherwise provoked, is not aggressive towards humans.

■ FAMILY 2 ■
HEMIGALEIDAE 4 genera

Chaenogaleus – 1 sp.

■ **C.MACROSTOMA**
Indonesian region. Grows to 1m (3ft).

Hemigaleus – 1 sp.

■ **H.MICROSTOMA**
NW Indian Ocean, Indonesia, Australia. Feeds almost exclusively on cephalopods. Grows to 1m (3ft).

Hemipristis – 1 sp.

■ **H.ELONGATUS** – Snaggletooth shark
Indian Ocean and W Pacific. Grows to 2.5m (8ft).

Paragaleus – 2 spp.

■ **P.PECTORALIS** – Atlantic Weasel shark
This is a coastal species from tropical West Africa. It is grey to bronze above and white below. A viviparous species, the number of young is unknown but they are about 40cm (16in) long at birth – a relatively large size, for the longest adult known is only 138cm (4½ft). They feed primarily on fishes, squids and crustaceans. Little is known about their biology.

■ **P.TENGI**
W Pacific. Poorly known. Grows to less than 1m (3ft).

■ FAMILY 3 ■
LEPTOCHARIIDAE 1 genus

Leptocharias – 1 sp.

■ **L.SMITHII** – Barbelled Houndshark
This is an example of a species that has had a common name thrust upon it by international decree. It is doubtful if anyone has ever actually referred to it as the Barbelled Houndshark. It is a small, slender species with a poorly differentiated lower caudal lobe; the axis of the upper lobe scarcely deviates from the body axis. A coastal species, it is found off West Africa and may extend as far north as the

Mediterranean. Becoming sexually mature at 60cm (2ft), it may reach a length of 80cm (2½ft) or more. The young are about 30–35cm (1ft) long at birth.

The species has had an unsettled taxonomic history. It was originally thought to be a member of the dogfish genus *Mustelus* (family Triakidae) but is now placed in its own family. It is not a rare fish but it is poorly known.

FAMILY 4

PROSCYLLIDAE 4 genera

Ctenacis – 1 sp.

■ *C.FEHLMANNI*
Known from only one example caught in deep water in NW Indian Ocean. 46cm (18in).

Eridacnis – 3 spp.

■ *E.BARBOURI*
Caribbean. Deep water. Grows to 30cm (12in).
■ *E.RADCLIFFEI*
Indian Ocean. Deep water. Grows to 25cm (10in).
■ *E.SINUANS*
SW Indian Ocean. Deep water. Grows to 37cm (14in).

Gollum – 1 sp.

■ *G.ATTENUATUS*
New Zealand. Deep water. Grows to 1m (3ft).

Proscyllium – 1 sp.

■ *P.HABERERI*
W Pacific. Deep water. Grows to 60cm (2ft).

FAMILY 5

PSEUDOTRIAKIDAE 1 genus

Pseudotriakis – 1 sp.

■ *P.MICRODON* – False Catshark
The False Catshark is widespread in deep seas close to the bottom at depths down to 1,500m (4,875ft). It is an elongated, almost eel-like, thin fish, dark grey to dark brown in colour. The spiracle is conspicuously large. Particularly diagnostic is the first dorsal fin. This has a long base, almost as long as the tail is. They feed on bottom-living fishes and invertebrates and have been photographed by remote-controlled cameras in the deep sea after coming within camera range to investigate the bait. They are ovoviviparous and one specimen has been recorded with two embryos which were about 90cm (3ft) long at birth. Females are slightly larger (almost 3m/10ft long) than the males (2.7m/9ft).

FAMILY 6

SCYLIORHINIDAE – 15 genera
Dogfishes (English) or Cat-sharks (American)

This speciose family contains, at the moment, 89 species of small to medium-sized sharks, many of which have conspicuous markings. 'Medium-sized' in this context means that few grow to more than 1m (3ft) in length, the majority to less. Adult sizes are given in the list below. They lack nasal barbels, have one anal fin and two spineless dorsal fins (usually), both short-based and set far back on the body. The teeth are small, numerous and multicuspid. They feed on midwater and bottom-living fishes, invertebrates and carrion. As far as is known, all are ovi-

Left ■ The False Catshark *Pseudotriakis microdon* taken off the Canary Islands; note the keel-like dorsal fin.

Above ■ Swellshark *Cephaloscyllium spp; the flaccid part of the body can be inflated with water to deter predators.*

parous. The empty egg-cases of coastal forms are often washed up on the shore after storms where they, together with the egg-cases of rays, have often been given the popular and romantic name of 'mermaid's purse'.

There are three centres of distribution of the species in this family. They are the western Pacific, the Australasian region, and the south-western Indian Ocean. Although the centres of dogfish species abundance are tropical, two species are the most common sharks in the north-western Atlantic and are important parts of the commercial catch.

Generally, English-speaking Europeans call the fishes 'dogfish' whereas Americans, South Africans and Antipodeans call them 'catsharks'. Rarely, Europeans do call them 'catsharks' but a proportion of the others may call catsharks 'dogfishes'. Dogfish, as a common name for these small sharks, originates with Pliny (AD 23–79) who called them *canicula*, or little dogs, in allusion to their habit of hunting in packs and biting fiercely. The origin of 'catshark' is less clear. In South Africa the Afrikaans name for them is *skaamoogs* or 'shy-eyes' because it seems that when caught they curl round to cover their eyes with their tails. Because cats often sleep like this, the name may have originated from that habit.

Aulohalaelurus – 1 sp.

■ *A.LABIOSUS*
W Australia. Grows to 70cm (2½ft).

Apristurus – 25 spp.

■ *A.ATLANTICUS*
SE Atlantic. Deep water. Grows to 25cm (10in).
■ *A.BRUNNEUS*
Central and NE Pacific. Deep water. Grows to 75cm (2½ft).

■ *A.CANUTUS*
Caribbean. Deep water. Grows to 50cm (1½ft).
■ *A.HERKLOTSI*
W Pacific. Deep water. Grows to less than 50cm (1½ft).
■ *A.INDICUS*
Indian Ocean. Deep water. Grows to 33cm (1ft).
■ *A.INVESTIGATORIS*
N Indian Ocean. Deep water. Grows to 25cm (10in).
■ *A.JAPONICUS*
NW Pacific. Deep water. Very common. Grows to 75cm (2½ft).
■ *A.KAMPAE*
NE and E Pacific. Deep water. Grows to 50cm (1½ft).
■ *A.LAURUSSONI*
Atlantic. Grows to under 75cm (2½ft).
■ *A.LONGICEPHALUS*
NW Pacific. Known from one example: 37cm (14in).
■ *A.MACRORHYNCHUS*
NW Pacific. Grows to 66cm (2ft).
■ *A.MADERENSIS*
SE Atlantic. Deep water. Grows to 66cm (2ft).
■ *A.MANIS*
N Atlantic. Grows to 90cm (3ft).
■ *A.MICROPS*
SE Atlantic. Grows to about 50cm (1½ft).
■ *A.NASUTUS*
SE Pacific. Deep water. Grows to 60cm (2ft).
■ *A.PARVIPINNIS*
S Pacific. Deep water. Grows to 50cm (1½ft).
■ *A.PLATYRHYNCHUS*
NW Pacific. Deep water. Grows to 75cm (2½ft).
■ *A.PROFUNDORUM*
NW Atlantic. As its trivial name implies, another inhabitant of deep water. In this case about 1,700m (5,500ft) down. Grows to 50cm (1½ft).
■ *A.RIVERI*
Caribbean. Deep water. Grows to 50cm (1½ft).
■ *A.SALDANHA*
SE Atlantic. Deep water. Grows to 75cm (2½ft).
■ *A.SIBOGAE*
W Pacific. Deep water. Known from one example: 21cm (8in).
■ *A.SINENSIS*
South China Sea. Known from an immature fish. 50cm (1½ft).
■ *A.PPONGICEPS*
W and S Pacific. Known from very few specimens. Deep water. Grows to 50cm (1½ft).
■ *A.STENSENI*
Central E Pacific. Deep water. Grows to 25cm (10in).
■ *A.VERWEYI*
Indonesia. Deep water. Only one specimen known. 30cm (1ft).

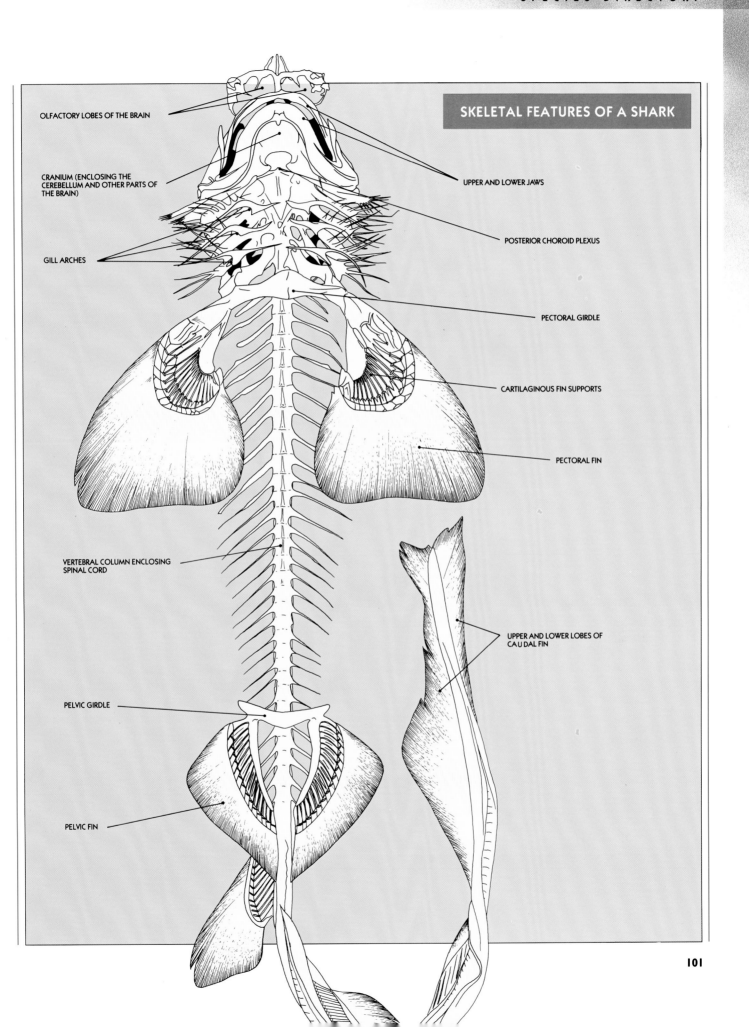

SKELETAL FEATURES OF A SHARK

OLFACTORY LOBES OF THE BRAIN

CRANIUM (ENCLOSING THE
CEREBELLUM AND OTHER PARTS OF
THE BRAIN)

GILL ARCHES

UPPER AND LOWER JAWS

POSTERIOR CHOROID PLEXUS

PECTORAL GIRDLE

CARTILAGINOUS FIN SUPPORTS

PECTORAL FIN

VERTEBRAL COLUMN ENCLOSING
SPINAL CORD

UPPER AND LOWER LOBES OF
CAUDAL FIN

PELVIC GIRDLE

PELVIC FIN

The above genus consists largely of small deep-water sharks. Many more species have been found, particularly in the North Pacific, as a result of deep-water exploratory trawling, especially by the Japanese. Photographs of new species have been published, and descriptions given, but they have not yet been given scientific names. The interested reader may find colour photographs of some specimens in the excellent series of books published by the Japan Fisheries Resource Conservation Association; the books are written in both Japanese and English. It can be confidently predicted that a list written in ten years' time will contain at least a dozen more species than the above list today. The deep waters of the world are poorly explored.

Above ■ The Nursehound *Scyliorhinus stellaris* (also known as the Greater or Larger Spotted dogfish or Bull Huss) lives mostly on rough or rocky grounds where it is frequently caught in deep-set nets.

Asymbolus – 2 spp.

■ *A.ANALIS*
S Australia. Shallow waters. Grows to 60cm (2ft).
■ *A.VINCENTI*
S Australia. Deeper water than *A. analis*. Grows to 60cm (2ft).
These two Catsharks, called respectively the Spotted Catshark and the Gulf Catshark, are widespread around the southern coasts of Australia. The former is light brown with dark brown spots; the latter is dark brown with white spots. They are much like the Spotted dogfish around European coasts.

Ateleomycterus – 2 spp.

■ *A.MACLEAYI*
Australia. Very shallow water. Grows to 60cm (2ft).
■ *A.MARMORATUS*
Indian Ocean. Shallow water. Grows to 70cm (2½ft).

Cephaloscyllium – Swell sharks 7 spp.

The common name of these medium-sized tropical sharks refers to their defence mechanism: they are able to inflate their bodies with air or with water to make themselves too large for a potential predator to swallow. All species are patterned, often with conspicuous saddle-like markings.

■ *C.FASCIATUM*
Australia. Deep water. Grows to about 1.5m (5ft).
■ *C.ISABELLUM*
Tropical W Pacific. Grows to about 1m (3ft).
This species is light brown in colour with much darker brown saddle-like or blotch-like markings. The southern representatives of this species have a more distinctly checkered pattern than the northern populations. New Zealanders say that this species makes a noise like a dog barking. If this description is accurate, the sound is probably involuntary, caused by the rapid passage of air during inflation or deflation. Sharks are not otherwise known to make noises.
■ *C.LATICEPS*
S Australia. Shallow water. Grows to 1m (3ft). This extremely sluggish species has a greatly extended spawning period: eggs are found during the entire first half of each year.
■ *C.NASCIONE*
Australia. Moderately deep water. Grows to 1m (3ft).
■ *C.SILASI*
N Indian Ocean. Grows to only 33cm (1ft).
■ *C.SUFFLANS*
SW Indian Ocean. Grows to 1m (3ft).
■ *C.VENTRIOSUM*
E Pacific Ocean. Grows to 1m (3ft). Very common off the Californian coast where it lives among the kelp beds. A sluggish, nocturnal species which has been bred in captivity. The young have enlarged, pointed denticles on the head to help them break out of the egg-case. The corners of the mouth are pleated to allow for the expansion of the body.

Cephalurus – 1 sp.

■ *C.CEPHALURUS*
Central E Pacific. Deep water. Grows to 30cm (1ft).

Galeus – 10 spp.

■ *G.ARAE* – Roughtail or Marbled Catshark
W Atlantic.
This species, which grows to about 50cm (1½ft) long, is widespread in deep waters in the western Atlantic. Over its range, however, there are distinct

Left ■ The Blackmouth dogfish
Galeus melastomus
occasionally ventures into
British coastal waters.

centres of abundance and it has been suggested that this species may be represented by discrete, dscontinuous populations or even subspecies. Something is known of the Caribbean population, which occurs at depths of 300–750m (975–2,450ft). As with some other sharks, there is segregation by size and sex. Young males live at the shallower end of the range, whereas mature males are found throughout the depth range. Immature females frequent the middle part of the range, and mature females from there downward. It is also likely that this population lays eggs whereas other populations have live young.

■ *G. BOARDMANI* – Sawtail shark
Australia. Grows to 66cm (2ft).

The common name of this probably oviparous species alludes to the row of saw-like denticles along the dorsal and ventral edges of the tail. It lives at depths between 40 and 100m (130–325ft) down.

■ *G. EASTMANI*
W Pacific. Deep water. Grows to 50cm (1½ft).

■ *G. MELASTOMUS* – Blackmouth Dogfish (Catshark)
E Atlantic. Grows to 1m (3ft).

This species ranges from north of Norway to Senegal, West Africa. It is widespread in the Mediterranean. Usually the eggs are laid in spring, but in the Mediterranean the dogfish breeds all the year round. The egg-cases, which do not have tendrils at the corners, are about 6×3cm (2½ × 1in). Those of the Mediterranean population are smaller.

It lives at depths from 200 to 800m (650–2,600ft), although at a lesser depth in the west and south of its range. It feeds on bottom-living and midwater fishes and invertebrates. In some areas it is extremely common.

■ *G. MURINUS*
NE Atlantic. Deep, cold, northern waters. Grows to less than 1m (3ft).
Possibly limited to waters around Iceland and the Faroe Islands.

■ *G. NIPPONENSIS*
NW Pacific. Deep water. Grows to just over 50cm (1½ft).

■ *G. PIPERATUS*
Central E Pacific. Deep water. Grows to 30cm (1ft).

■ *G. POLLI*
African Atlantic. Deep water. Grows to 40cm (16in).

■ *G. SAUTERI*
NW Pacific. Bottom-dweller in offshore waters. Grows to less than 50cm (1½ft).

■ *G. SCHULTZI*
W Pacific. Deep water. Grows to 40cm (16in)+.

Halaelurus – 11 spp.

Members of this genus are bottom-dwellers of the Indopacific region. In some areas they are regarded as sport fish; in other areas they are considered a nuisance. To add to the confusion regarding common names, the official common name of *Halaelurus natalensis* is Tiger Catshark, but this appellation is very rarely used in the areas in which it is common, where it is known just as the Dogfish.

■ *H. ALCOCKI*
NW Indian Ocean. Deep water. Grows to 30cm (1ft).

■ *H. BOESEMANI*
Indian Ocean and Australasia. Grows to 50cm (1½ft).

■ *H. BUERGERI*
West Pacific. Grows to 50cm (1½ft).

■ *H.CANESCENS*
SE Pacific. Deep water. Grows to 75cm (2½ft).

■ *H.DAWSONI*
New Zealand. Deep water. Grows to less than 50cm (1½ft).

■ *H.HISPIDUS*
N Indian Ocean. Deep water. Grows to 30cm (1ft).

■ *H.IMMACULATUS*
W Pacific. Deep water. Grows to 75cm (2½ft).

■ *H.LINEATUS*
SW Indian Ocean. From shallows to deep sea. Grows to 50cm (1½ft).

■ *H.LUTARIUS*
SW Indian Ocean. Deep waters, most frequently on a silty bottom. Grows to 40cm (16in).

■ *H.NATALENSIS* – Tiger Catshark
Bottom-dweller, inshore waters. Grows to 50cm (1½ft).

■ *H.QUAGGA*
W and N Indian Ocean. Grows to 35cm (14in).

Haploblepharus – 3 spp.

Sometimes called Shysharks because they cover their heads with their tails when caught:

■ *H.EDWARDSII*
SW Indian Ocean. Shallow waters. Grows to 60cm (2ft).

■ *H.FUSCUS*
SW Indian Ocean. Shallow waters. Grows to 70cm (2½ft).

■ *H.PICTUS*
SE Atlantic and SW Indian Ocean. Grows to over 50cm (1½ft).

Holohalaelurus – 2 spp.

■ *H.PUNCTATUS*
SW Indian Ocean. Grows to 35cm (1ft).

■ *H.REGANI*
W and N Indian Ocean. Grows to over 50cm (1½ft).

Parmaturus – 4 spp.

■ *P.CAMPECHIENSIS*
Gulf of Mexico. Adult size unknown: the only specimen ever caught is a juvenile.

■ *P.MELANOBRANCHIUS*
W Pacific. Deep water. Grows to 85cm (3ft).

■ *P.PILOSUS*
NW Pacific. Grows to 60cm (2ft).

■ *P.XANIURUS*
NE and central Pacific. Deep water. Grows to 60cm (2ft). Apart from a specimen of a juvenile *P. campechiensis* from the Gulf of Mexico (the validity of

the placement of this specimen within the genus is dubious) these sharks are bottom-dwellers of the northern Pacific. They have a soft skin, often seeming to be loose. There is a strong tendency for these species to have a large gill region, an attribute that has been interpreted as an adaptation for living in waters with a low oxygen content.

Pentanchus – 1 sp.

■ *P.PROFUNDICOLUS*
W Pacific. Only one known: 50cm (1½ft).
As currently defined, and identified from a single specimen of its genus, this shark is the only species within the order of Carcharhiniformes that has only dorsal fin, rather than two. The specimen was carefully examined and there was no sign of physical damage. At various times other species (all with two dorsal fins) have been included in *Pentanchus*, but have subsequently been considered to fit better into other genera. The questions now remaining are whether the only specimen attributable to this genus is or is not a genetically abnormal specimen of something else, and whether or not *Pentanchus* is therefore a valid genus. The discovery of more specimens conspecific with that referred to *Pentanchus profundicolus* may solve the problem.

Poroderma – 3 spp.

■ *P. AFRICANUM* – Striped Catshark
South African inshore waters. Grows to 1m (3ft).

■ *P. MARLEYI*
SW Indian Ocean. Poorly known. Grows to 60cm (2ft)+.

■ *P. PANTHERIUM* – Leopard Catshark
South African inshore waters. Grows to 75cm (2½ft). The Leopard Catshark has very pantherine ocelli – tyre markings – and the Striped Catshark has three or four dark brown longitudinal stripes. These are sluggish species of inshore waters, and are considered a nuisance by South African anglers.

Schroederichthys – 4 spp.

■ *S. BIVIUS*
SE Pacific. Grows to 70cm (2ft).

■ *S. CHILENSIS*
SE Pacific. Shallow waters. Grows to 60cm (2ft).

■ *S. MACULATUS*
Caribbean. Deep water. Grows to 35cm (14in).

■ *S. TENUIS*
SW Atlantic. Deep waters especially off Brazil. Grows to 70cm (2ft).

Scyliorhinus – 13 spp.

■ *S. BESNARDI*
SW Atlantic. Bottom-dweller. Grows to 50cm (1½ft).

■ *S. BOA*
Caribbean. Grows to 50cm (1½ft).

■ *S. CANICULA* – Lesser Spotted Dogfish

Despite official attempts to force the 'accepted' common name of Smallspotted Catshark on this species, it is still known in vernacular English as the Lesser Spotted Dogfish.

This small shark, rarely growing to 1m (3ft) in length, is among the best-known of all fishes to biologists. For several generations most biologists have gleaned their understanding of basic vertebrate anatomy from dissecting this species. Although they have never been caught specifically for that purpose, many of those caught inadvertently along with more commercially desirable species have found their way ultimately on to a dissecting board. For that reason its anatomy is known in great detail.

It is a common species, living on or near the bottom from shallow water to depths of about 100m (325ft), except in the Mediterranean Sea, where they live at greater depths, down to 400m (1,300ft). Being both common and hardy the species is frequently kept in aquaria, where it thrives. In captivity it has been the subject of many physiological experiments. It has even been observed mating in aquaria. In some areas its biology in nature is much less of a mystery than that of other sharks.

Scyliorhinus canicula lives along the coasts of the north-eastern Atlantic from Scandinavia down to Senegal and in the Mediterranean. Most of its life is spent close to the bottom, where it feeds largely on molluscs and crustaceans. Scallops, whelks, razorshells, swimming crabs, hermit crabs, small lobsters, shrimps and prawns are especially favoured. Small bottom-living fish are eaten as, less frequently, are some midwater fish. The teeth are small and numerous.

During copulation, the male winds completely round the female's body so that his head crosses over his tail. The female later lays about 20 eggs and scatters them among seaweed or any other form of environment on which the tendrils on the eggs can become caught. The eggs are about 5 × 11cm (2 × 4½in), rectangular, and have rough cases. At each corner is a flexible tendril which when fully extended may be 1m (3ft) long. The tendrils coil up, however, to about 10cm or so in length. They hold the egg fast for the 8–9 months it takes for the embryo to develop. The egg-case allows gas exchange to take place,

Left ■ The Lesser Spotted dogfish *Scyliorhinus canicula* is nocturnal and may be encountered during the day by divers lying 'asleep' on the seabed.

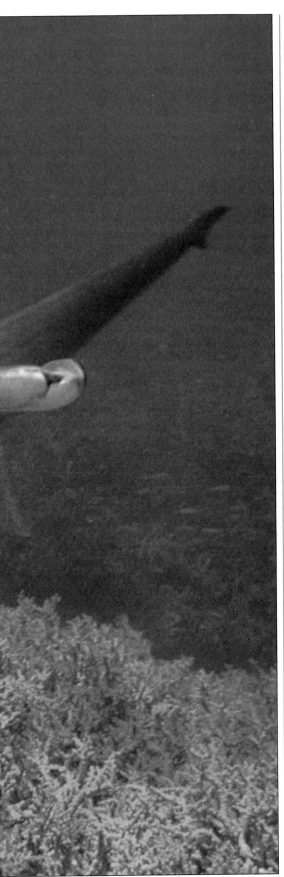

thereby facilitating the respiration of the developing embryo. The young are about 10cm (4in) long when they break free of the egg-case.

The newly hatched young have diagonal dark stripes; the adult is pale brown with darker brown spots.

■ *S.CAPENSIS*
SW Indian Ocean. Grows to over 1m (3ft).

■ *S.CERVIGONI*
West Africa. Deep water. Grows to 75cm (2½ft).

■ *S.GARMANI*
W Pacific. Poorly known. A small species.

■ *S.HAECKELII*
SW Atlantic. Poorly known. Grows to about 50cm (1½ft).

■ *S.HESPERIUS*
Caribbean. Deep water. Grows to about 50cm (1½ft).

■ *S.MEADI*
W and NW Atlantic. Grows to about 50cm (1½ft).

■ *S.RETIFER* – Chain Catshark (Dogfish)
This North Atlantic species is found from New Jersey to the Carolinas. Marked with a chain-like dark pattern (as its common name suggests), it is slightly smaller than the European Lesser Spotted Dogfish, a species that in other ways it resembles. The Chain Dogfish is, in many ecological ways, the American equivalent of *Scyliorhinus canicula*.

■ *S.STELLARIS* – Greater Spotted Dogfish or Nurse-hound
This species is much like a large Lesser Spotted Dogfish. The spots are fewer and larger than in that species. Overall, its range is like that of its close relative but it tends to be much scarcer in the north. The diet is also similar except that the Greater Spotted Dogfish feeds on a wider range of fishes – including the Lesser Spotted Dogfish. It may reach 1.75m (5½ft) in length and achieve a weight of 10kg (22lb). Its biology is not well known.

■ *S.TORAZAME*
Australasia. Grows to 50cm (1½ft).

■ *S.TORREI*
Caribbean region. Deep water. Grows to 35cm (1ft).

■■■■ FAMILY 7 ■■■■

SPHRYNIDAE – 2 genera
Hammerhead and Bonnethead sharks

Behind the greatly modified head, the Hammerhead sharks have a body that is carcharinid in nature. All their extreme features are found in the front of the fish.

Teeth like those of the living Hammerheads have been found in late Eocene deposits, so this extremely adapted group may have an ancient lineage.

Left ■ *Sphyrna mokarran* – the Great Hammerhead shark; the advantage of the peculiar shaped head of hammerheads is not known, for certain, though there are several hypotheses which may explain its function.

Eusphyra – 1 sp.

■ *E. BLOCHII*

N Indian Ocean to Australia. Shallow waters. Grows to 1.5m (5ft).

The head of *Eusphyra* is the widest of all the Hammerheads; its width may be nearly half of the body length. It has fewer vertebrae than other members of the family, and nostrils that are not at the front corners of the head but are between the eyes and the midline.

Sphyrna – 8 spp.

■ *S. CORONA*

E and SE Pacific. Grows to less than 1m (3ft).

■ *S. COUARDI*

SE Atlantic. Coastal waters. Grows to 3m (10ft). It has white-tipped pectoral fins.

■ *S. LEWINI*

Worldwide in all seas except the coldest. Grows to over 4m (13ft).

■ *S. MEDIA*

Tropical E Pacific and W Atlantic. Shallow waters. Grows to 1.5m (5ft).

■ *S. MOKARRAN*

Almost all temperate and tropical seas. Reef dweller. The largest of the hammerheads, it grows occasionally to more than 6m (20ft).

■ *S. TIBURO* – Bonnethead

Tropical E Pacific and W Atlantic. Grows to about 1.5m (5ft).

■ *S. TUDES*

SW Atlantic. Shallow waters. Grows to 1.5m (5ft).

■ *S. ZYGAENA*

Worldwide. The largest hammerhead. The adult grows to almost 4m (13ft).

Although most species are tropical, *Sphyrna zygaena* has been found as far north as the southern North Sea on the eastern side of the Atlantic – indeed it is not that uncommon in the English Channel in summer – and to the level of Nova Scotia on the west. On occasions they make the northward journey in large shoals. Off the Canadian coast they stay in northern waters until the temperature drops to below about 20°C (68°F), when they move southward.

All the species, no matter how extensive their range, undertake seasonal movements, swimming polewards in their respective hemispheric summers and equatorwards in their respective winters.

On top of the seasonal movements, which are entirely comprehensible, at least one species – the Bonnethead (*S. tiburo*) – has a less comprehensible behaviour pattern. At seemingly irregular times, unrelated to the season of the year, phases of the moon, or any other factors investigated, in certain areas they gather together in dense shoals at the surface. The complete randomness of this activity both in time and area has led to no conclusions at all about its purpose. The only common factor noted is that all the fish in the shoal are the same size.

The daily behaviour of the commonest Hammerhead (*S. lewini*) has been studied. During the day they swim in shoals of about 100 fishes. In these shoals the females are much more numerous than the males. Despite this, mating has never been observed in these shoals. The purpose of these diurnal shoals is unknown; it is not for protection, for they have no natural enemies, and it is not for more efficient feeding – they do not feed during the day. At night the shoals disperse and the fish swim off singly to feed.

The distribution of some species of Hammerheads is another puzzle. For example, *S. tiburo* and *S. media* live in both the eastern Pacific and the western Atlantic (ie both sides of the Americas), but the former has the greater range. In the Pacific population of *S. tiburo* there is a tendency for the shark's head to be slightly broader and more pointed than in the Atlantic population. The degree of difference, however, is not considered to be enough to regard the two isolated populations as different species. An explanation put forward to explain the distribution is that the species was found over that region before the barrier that is now Central America formed and the slight differences in head shape have developed since that time.

The function or purpose of the peculiar head is unknown. It is likely that the lateral expansion of the head – the 'wings' – act as hydrofoils ... but other sharks function as efficiently without this feature. The eyes are at the tips of the 'wings' and it could be that the widely spaced eyes allow the fish to gain a better appreciation of distance. As the head swings from side to side in swimming, the nostrils sample a greater volume of water than they would otherwise do – so could the enhanced opportunity to use its sense of smell be a purpose of the head shape? Because the head is widened, the electro-sensitive ampullae of Lorenzini cover a greater area, and this may enable the hammerhead to detect its prey more efficiently. We do not know. Any combination of these suggestions (or none of them) may be the evolutionary 'reason' for the expanded head.

Although Hammerheads have large brains for a shark (as do other carcharinids), the brain size is not affected by the head extensions.

Side view of an immature *Sphyrna tiburo*, the bonnethead.

Hammerheads feed mostly on fishes (both bottom-living and pelagic) and invertebrates. It appears they are particularly partial to rays, especially the sting ray. One Hammerhead, 4m (13ft) long, caught off the eastern seaboard of the USA, had 54 sting ray spines embedded in its mouth.

Hammerheads are viviparous. They have large litters. Both within and between species there is a general rule that the larger the female, the greater the number of pups. More than 40 pups have been found in a very large female. The young are born head first, and the 'wings' of the head are folded back to make their passage into the world easier for them and their mother.

In the same regions they have been hunted for food and for their liver oil, which contains a great concentration of Vitamin A.

Larger hammerheads have been implicated in attacks on humans. In such cases there can be no doubt about the identity of the shark involved. These attacks can, however, pertinently be put into perspective by the words of an expert on these fishes, Sr Carvallo, written in 1967: 'S. zygaena is the most familiar and probably the most dangerous when attacked by harpoon or fish spear, often charging the boat head-on and capsizing it.'

FAMILY 8

TRIAKIDAE – 9 genera

Topes and Smoothhounds

Triakids are a family of medium-sized sharks almost worldwide in their distribution. The largest rarely grows to much over 2m (6½ft) in length. Most are substantially smaller. The widely used common name 'Smoothhound' refers to the absence of spines in front of the median fins. For some reason that is unclear, several species of triakids throughout the world have acquired the common name of Sweet William; the oldest use of that name, probably alluding to the Tope, dates from 1730. All the triakids given this name have a strong smell of an ammoniacal nature, especially when not extremely fresh. Although the identity of the William so insulted has not been satisfactorily explained, it seems likely that it alludes to William of Orange (1688–1702).

Much like other carcharinids in most features, triakids are characterized by the possession of very small teeth arranged in many rows for the crushing of small invertebrates on which many of them feed.

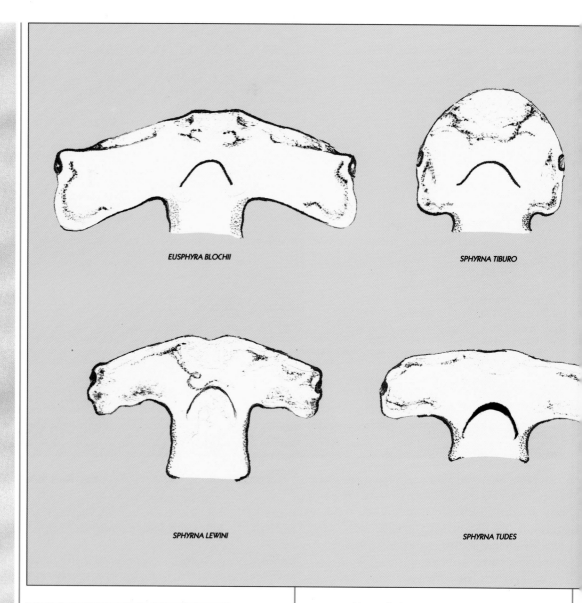

EUSPHYRA BLOCHII

SPHYRNA TIBURO

SPHYRNA LEWINI

SPHYRNA TUDES

Furgaleus – 1 sp.

■ *F. MACKI*

Australia. Bottom-dweller at some depth. Grows to 1.5m (5ft).

Galeorhinus – 1 sp.

■ *G. GALEUS* – Tope

Temperate waters of all oceans. May grow to 2m (6½ft).

The tope is an inhabitant of temperate and sub-tropical oceans. Although widespread, its distribution is patchy and it does not seem to be present in the north-western Atlantic nor north-western Pacific.

There is still uncertainty whether 'the tope' is one or several species; the matter is under review at the moment. Here all the nominal 'species' (eg *Galeorhinus australis* of Australia and *Galeorhinus zyopterus* of the eastern Pacific) are regarded as one single species.

In the north-eastern Atlantic, Tope grow to over 2m (6½ft) long and are eagerly sought by anglers. They tend to move inshore in summer and out into deeper water in winter. During the summer, small adults may be very close to the shore in extremely shallow water. They mostly live on or near the bottom (gravel or sandy substrate is favoured) at depths down to 60m (200ft). They feed on small fishes – largely whiting, codling and flat fishes – but occasionally consume invertebrates. Up to 40, but most frequently about 20, young are born to each mother in the summer. The pups from a large mother are about 40cm (16in) long at birth after a gestation of one year.

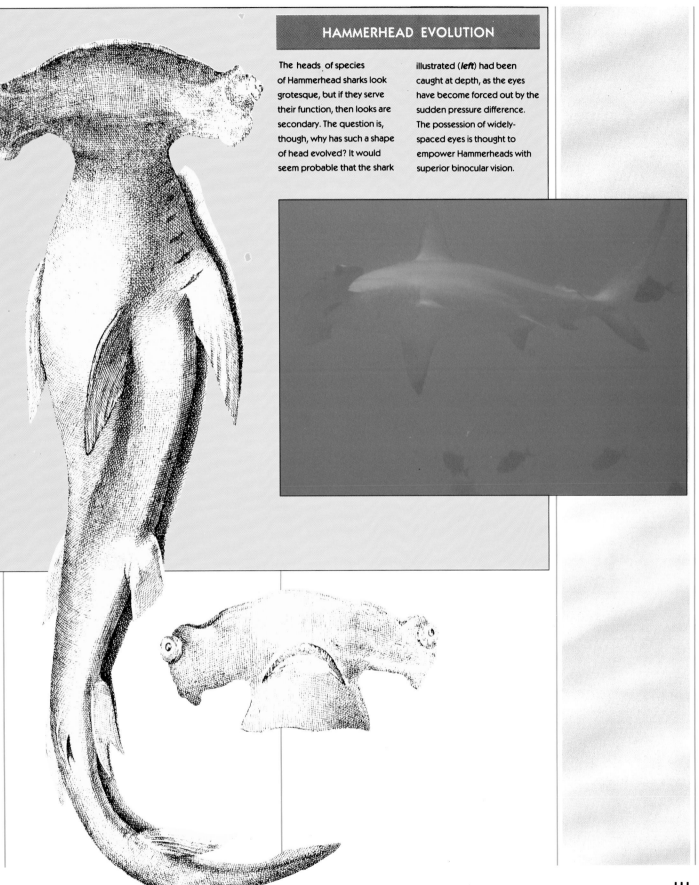

HAMMERHEAD EVOLUTION

The heads of species of Hammerhead sharks look grotesque, but if they serve their function, then looks are secondary. The question is, though, why has such a shape of head evolved? It would seem probable that the shark illustrated (*left*) had been caught at depth, as the eyes have become forced out by the sudden pressure difference. The possession of widely-spaced eyes is thought to empower Hammerheads with superior binocular vision.

Research in Australia has shown that in their Tope population only about half the mature females are gravid in any one year. The number of pups varied from 17 to 41, with an average number of 28. The pups were some 30cm (1ft) long at birth and had had a gestation of only six months. Growth is slow. Males mature at 140cm (4½ft) when ten years old. The Australian (and Californian) populations form dense shoals, whereas the Atlantic tope are much less gregarious.

The Californian population has been much exploited for its fins which are used in soup.

Gogolia – 1 sp.

■ **G. FILEWOODI**
Known from only one individual, 74cm (2½ft) long, caught in deep water off Papua New Guinea.

Hemitriakis – 2 spp.

■ **H. JAPANICA**
W and NW Pacific. Grows to 1.25m (4ft).
■ **H. LEUCOPERIPTERA**
W Pacific. Grows to 1m (3ft).

Hypogaleus – 1 sp.

■ **H. HYUGAENSIS** – Lesser Soupfin shark
Indian and W Pacific Oceans. Grows to 1.25m (4ft).

Iago – 2 spp.

■ **I. GARRICKI**
Very localized in W Pacific. Poorly known. Deep water. Grows to 75cm (2½ft).
■ **I. OMANENSIS**
NW Indian Ocean. Deep water. Grows to about 50cm (1½ft).

Mustelus – 20 spp.

■ **M. ANTARCTICUS** – Sweet William
Australia. Grows to 1.5m (5ft).
■ **M. ASTERIAS** – Starry Smoothhound or Sweet William

E Atlantic and Mediterranean. Grows to 1.5m (5ft). The Starry Smoothhound is very similar to the Smoothhound (see below). Both species are found around the coasts of north-western Europe, but this species extends further out to sea and further north than the Smoothhound. As its names implies, its grey-brown ground colour is spattered with numerous white spots, which are absent in the Smoothhound. It is ovoviviparous, about 20 young being born at a time, each about 30cm (1ft) long. By contrast the Smoothhound is viviparous.

■ **M. CALIFORNICUS**
E Pacific. Grows to over 1m (3ft).

■ *M.CANIS*
W Atlantic. Grows to 1.5m (5ft). The west Atlantic equivalent to the very similar east Atlantic *M. asterias* and *M. mustelus*. Extremely common off the USA.

■ *M.DORSALIS*
E and SE Pacific. Shallow water. Grows to less than 75cm (2½ft).

■ *M.FASCIATUS*
SW Atlantic. Shallow waters. Grows to 1.25m (4ft).

■ *M.GRISEUS*
W and NW Pacific. Grows to 1m (3ft).

■ *M.HENLEI*
E Pacific. Common in shallow water. Grows to 1m (3ft).

■ *M.HIGMANI*
SW Atlantic. Bottom-dweller. Grows to less than 75cm (2½ft).

■ *M.LENTICULATUS*
New Zealand. Bottom-dweller at many depths. Grows to 1.25m (4ft).

■ *M.LUNULATUS*
NE and central Pacific. Common. Grows to 1.75m (5½ft).

■ *M.MANAZO*
Parts of Indian and W Pacific Oceans. Common off Japan. Grows to just over 1m (3ft).

■ *M.MENTO*
Off southern South America. Grows to 1.25m (4ft).

■ *M.MOSIS*
W and N Indian Ocean. Grows to 1.5m (5ft).

■ *M.MUSTELUS* – Smoothhound or Sweet William
E Atlantic and Mediterranean. Grows to 1.5m (5ft). (See also *M. asterias*)

■ *M.NORRISI*
SW Atlantic and Caribbean. Grows to 1m (3ft).

■ *M.PALUMBES*
South African waters. Grows to about 1m (3ft).

■ *M.PUNCTULATUS*
Mediterranean and W African seas. Grows to over 75cm (2½ft).

■ *M.SCHMITTI*
SW Atlantic. Grows to 75cm (2½ft).

■ *M.WHITNEYI*
SE Pacific. Grows to over 75cm (2½ft).

Scylliogaleus – 1 sp.

■ *S.QUECKETTI*
South African shallow waters. Grows to 1m (3ft).

Triakis – 5 spp.

This seemingly obscure genus gave its name to this entire family of sharks when the family was renamed to avoid confusion with a group of mammals. The most significant genus in the family (in the sense of comprising the most species, being the most familiar, and having the widest distribution) is *Mustelus*, and in older reference works the family containing this genus was accordingly known as the Mustelidae. Far too late it was realized that the name Mustelidae had for even longer been used to describe the mammal family that includes the weasels, stoats, minks, otters and polecats. The shark family was then renamed Triakidae.

■ *T.ACUTIPINNA*
Only two specimens known, from off Ecuador. Grows to 1m (3ft).

■ *T.MACULATA*
SE Pacific. Grows to 1.75m (5½ft).

■ *T.MEGALOPTERUS* – Gully shark or Sweet William (see also *Mustelus antarcticus*)
South African waters. Grows to 1.75m (5½ft).

■ *T.SCYLLIUM*
NW Pacific. Bottom-dweller in shallow water. Grows to 1.5m (5ft).

■ *T.SEMIFASCIATA* – Leopard shark
N and NE Pacific. Grows to 1.75m (5½ft).
The Leopard shark is common on the western American seaboard. It is a sluggish species, feeding largely on molluscs. Prettily marked and docile, it is often kept in aquaria. There is one record of this mollusc-eating, sluggish species molesting a diver; fortunately, the diver was able to beat off the 1m/3ft-long 'attacker'. Both diver and shark were unhurt.

SQUALIFORMES
(Dogfish, Gulper sharks and
Sleeper sharks)

This order, of three families, lacks the anal fin which distinguishes it from all other orders of 'shark-like' sharks. The other two orders lacking the anal fin have either flattened bodies or a 'saw-like' rostrum.

Below ■ Two small sharks from the northwestern Pacific: (upper) *Mustelus manazo* the Starspotted Smoothhound; (lower) *Hemitriakis japanica* the Japanese topeshark.

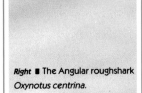

Right ■ The Angular roughshark *Oxynotus centrina*.

■■■ FAMILY 1 ■■■

ECHINORHINIDAE – Bramble sharks 1 genus

This family derives its common name from the presence of a few, greatly enlarged, thorn-like denticles.

Echinorhinus – 2 spp.

■ *E.BRUCUS* – Bramble shark
Most parts of the Atlantic, Indian Ocean, W Pacific, Australasia.
The Bramble (or Briar, Spinous or Spiny) shark is a bottom-dweller in cooler waters. The two dorsal fins, pelvic fins and the thick caudal fin are set close together. This configuration of fins, transferring the major thrust for swimming to the rear of the body, is usually found in fishes that are sluggish but specialize in short bursts of very rapid acceleration to catch their prey. This 'lurking predator' body form is exemplified by the pike in fresh water. Probably, therefore, the Bramble shark has the abilities typical of a lurking predator. It is known to feed on fishes and crabs.

Its method of reproduction is unknown, but it is probably ovoviviparous. One specimen, caught on a line set for conger eels off south-western England on 1 January, 1869, contained 17 eggs. Dogfishes were found in its stomach. Occasional specimens are inadvertently caught on baited long lines. When landed, they have been described as tenacious of life, sometimes still alive and active 10 hours after the hook has been removed and the fish left on the deck of the boat.

Found mostly at depths of 400–900m (1,300–2,900ft), they are brown in colour.
■ *E.COOKEI* – Prickle shark
E Pacific, Australia. Grows to about 4m (13ft).

■■■ FAMILY 2 ■■■

OXYNOTIDAE

This family contains distinctive hump-backed sharks with high, expansive dorsal fins. Stout spines supporting dorsal fins are embedded in the fin tissue. The body is triangular in cross-section.

Although these sharks are conspicuous, very little is known about their biology. *Oxynotus paradoxus* is believed to be about 25cm (10in) long at birth, and *O. centrina* is about 50cm (20in) at maturity. This genus is being studied by researchers in Spain, and it is as a result of their work that the colour illustrations here can be published for the first time.

Oxynotus – 4 spp.

■ *O.BRUNENSIS*
Australia and New Zealand. Bottom-dweller in moderately deep water. Grows to 75cm (2½ft).
■ *O.CARIBBAEUS*
Caribbean. Deep water. Grows to 50cm (20in).

Left ■ Taiwan Gulper shark
Centrophorus niaukang. The
species was originally known
from the China Sea, but
recently it has been recorded
in the northeast Atlantic.

■ **O.** *CENTRINA*
E Atlantic and Mediterranean. Grows to 1.5m (5ft).

■ **O.** *PARADOXUS* – Humantin
E Atlantic (not Mediterranean). Grows to 1.25m (4ft).

■■■■■ FAMILY 3 ■■■■■

SQUALIDAE 16 genera

This family includes the world's smallest shark.

Aculeola – 1 sp.

■ **A.** *NIGRA*
SE Pacific. Deep water. Grows to 60cm (2ft).

Centrophorus – 9 spp.

Most species have large green eyes.
■ **C.** *ACUS*
Caribbean and NW Pacific. Deep water. Grows to 80cm (2½ft). The peculiar recorded distribution suggests it may remain unobserved at many intermediate localities.
■ **C.** *GRANULOSUS* – Gulper shark
Most of the Atlantic to the SW Indian Ocean. Deep water. Grows to 1.5m (5ft).
In this poorly-known deep-water species the dorsal fins are not as conspicuously long-based at they are in most members of the genus. Adults are dark grey to greyish brown above, paler ventrally, but the young are grey and their fins have white edges. They are ovoviviparous and feed on fishes and squids. There is, as with many squaliform sharks, a tendency for the teeth of the upper and lower jaws to be dissimilar.
■ **C.** *HARRISONI*
SE Australia. Deep water. Grows to 80cm (2½ft).
■ **C.** *LUSITANICUS*
E Atlantic and W Indian Ocean. Grows to 1.5m (5ft).
■ **C.** *MOLUCCENSIS*
Parts of the Indian and Pacific Oceans. Common in the SW Indian Ocean. Grows to about 1m (3ft).
■ **C.** *NIAUKANG*
NW Pacific (Taiwan area). Deep water. Grows to 1.5m (5ft).
■ **C.** *SQUAMOSUS*
W Atlantic, Indian Ocean, Australasia. Deep water. Grows to 1.5m (5ft).
■ **C.** *TESSELLATUS*
NW Pacific. Grows to less than 1m (3ft).
■ **C.** *UYATO*
W Mediterranean, SE and E Atlantic, Gulf of Mexico, off southern Mozambique, Taiwan. Deep water. Grows to 1m (3ft). Another apparently oddly distributed species.

Centroscyllium – 6 spp.

A genus of luminescent sharks. Their teeth have three to five cusps.

■ C.FABRICII
West coast of Africa and polar waters. Grows to less than 1m (3ft). Ovoviviparous. Another odd distribution.

■ C.GRANULATUM
SW Atlantic. Deep water. Grows to 30cm (1ft).

■ C.KAMOHARAE
NW Pacific. Deep water. Grows to 50cm (20in).

■ C.CREPIDATER
E and NE Atlantic, New Zealand. Ovoviviparous. Fish eater. Grows to 90cm (3ft).

■ C.CRYPTACANTHUS
S Atlantic and Madeira. Deep water. Grows to about 1m (3ft).

■ C.MACRACANTHUS
Only known from one specimen: 68cm (2ft 2½in)

Right ■ Centroscymnus owstoni; a deep water shark, like all species of the genus.

■ C.NIGRUM
Central and S Pacific. Deep water. Grows to about 50cm (20in).

■ C.ORNATUM
N Indian Ocean. Deep water. Grows to 50cm (20in).

■ C.RITTERI
NW Pacific. Deep water. Grows to less than 50cm (20in).

Centroscymnus – 6 spp.

Fish of this genus are distinguished from the previous species in that their teeth have only a single cusp.

■ C.COELOLEPIS
ENE and NE Atlantic. Very deep, cool waters.
C. coelolepis is sometimes called the Portuguese shark. One specimen has provided very detailed information about the depth at which it lives. Normally, the depth at which deep-sea fish are caught is vague because there is no indication whether they have been caught as the net was on the way down, or the way up. However, one Portuguese shark was caught in a trap set on the bottom at 2,718m (8,922ft). Because the trap was closed when travelling vertically, the precise depth is not in doubt. This is the deepest accurate record for a shark, although species as yet undetermined have been photographed at greater depths (over 4,300m/14,000ft) and other species may well have been recovered from greater, but imprecise, depths.

It is a dark brown fish living in waters at 5–6°C (41–43°F), and is known to feed on fishes. It is ovoviviparous, 13–16 young being born at a time, each about 20cm (8in) long.

long, caught in the Straits of Magellan off Tierra del Fuego.

■ C.OWSTONI
W Pacific to New Zealand, Caribbean. Deep water. Grows to 80cm (2½ft).

■ C.PLUNKETI
Australia and New Zealand. Deep water. Grows to 1.75m (5½ft).

Cirrhigaleus – 1 sp.

■ C.BARBIFER
NW Pacific to New Zealand. Bottom-dweller in deep water. Grows to 1.25m (4ft).

Dalatias – 1 sp.

■ D.LICHIA – Darkie Charlie
Widespread, apart from the poles and E Pacific. Deep water. Grows to 1.75m (5½ft).
This widespread species is found at depths from 90 to 1,000m (300 to 3,250ft) but is most abundant at depths between 300 and 600m (1,000 to 2,000ft). The teeth of the upper and lower jaws are markedly dissimilar. Those of the lower jaw are broad-based with a triangular blade that has serrated edges. The upper jaw teeth are lanceolate, and curve inwards. It is a fish eater and often has fast-swimming fishes in its stomach. Records of specimens caught so far show that a male's stomach is generally fuller than a female's. It has been suggested that during the catching the females may regurgitate their food more easily than the males.

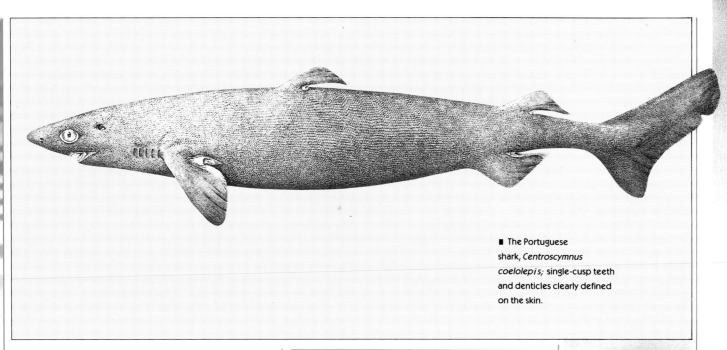

■ The Portuguese shark, *Centroscymnus coelolepis;* single-cusp teeth and denticles clearly defined on the skin.

It is ovoviviparous; 10–16 pups are born at a time, each about 30cm (1ft) long. There seems to be no well-defined breeding season.

Deania – 4 spp.

A poorly known genus of deep-sea sharks. They have a long beak-like snout, and in all species the teeth of the upper and lower jaws are different, and there is a further difference between the teeth of males and those of females.

Where known, they live at depths from 400 to 1,000m (1,300 to 3,250ft). They are grey to dark brown in colour. The diet is unknown but is probably fishes. They are thought, at least in the case of *Deania calcea*, to be ovoviviparous, the young being less than 30cm long at birth.

■ *D.CALCEA*
Antitropical temperate waters and warm, deep waters. Grows to over 1m (3ft).

■ *D.HISTRICOSA*
Madeira and Japanese deep waters. Grows to over 1m (3ft).

■ *D.PROFUNDORUM*
This is a controversial species. If all specimens attributed to it have been correctly identified, it occurs in deep waters in the north-western and south-eastern Atlantic, the south-western Indian Ocean and around the Philippines. They grow to 75cm (2½ft).

■ *D.QUADRISPINOSUM*
SE Atlantic, SW Indian Ocean and south coasts of Australia. Deep water. Grows to nearly 1.25m (4ft).

Etmopterus – 17 spp.

In this genus of small deep-sea sharks the teeth of the upper jaw have 3–7 cusps whereas the lower-jaw teeth are broader and unicuspid. In all species, glands in the skin secrete a luminous slime that has been described as glowing golden-yellow or blue-green. The skin feels smooth and velvety to the touch.

■ *E.BAXTERI*
New Zealand. Bottom-dweller in deep water. Grows to over 1m (3ft).

■ *E.BRACHYURUS*
W Pacific. Deep water. Another contender for the title of smallest shark. Grows to about 25cm (10in).

■ *E.BULLISI*
NW Atlantic and Caribbean. Only immature specimens so far known.

■ *E.DECACUSPIDATUS*
W Pacific. Known from just one fish 29cm (11in) long.

■ *E.GRACILISPINIS*
SE, SW and NW Atlantic. Bottom-dweller at moderate depths; midwater inhabitant in deeper waters. Grows to 33cm (1ft).

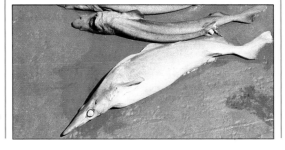

Left ■ The Birdbeak dogfish, *Deania calcea,* a curiosity from deep waters.

■ *E.GRANULOSUS*

SE Pacific, SE and SW Atlantic. Grows to 40cm (16in)+.

■ *E.HILLIANUS*

NW Atlantic and Caribbean. Grows to 50cm (1½ft).

■ *E.LUCIFER*

SW Atlantic, SW Indian Ocean, W Pacific to Australasia. Deep water. Grows to almost 50cm (1½ft).

■ *E.POLLI*

SE Atlantic. Grows to 25cm (10in).

■ *E.PRINCEPS*

NE, NW and SE Atlantic. Grows to 75cm (2½ft).

■ *E.PUSILLUS*

E Atlantic, central and SW Atlantic, Japan. Grows to 75cm (2½ft).

This species is found at a wide range of depths from 300 to 1,000m (1,000 to 3,250ft). Further observation may well reveal that it is more widespread than believed at the moment. It feeds on fishes and cephalopods. It is probably ovoviviparous. The size at birth is unknown, but specimens 50cm (1½ft) long are still immature.

■ *E.SCHULTZI*

Caribbean. Grows to 30cm (1ft).

■ *E.SENTOSUS*

SW Indian Ocean. Only immature fish known: 27cm (11in)+.

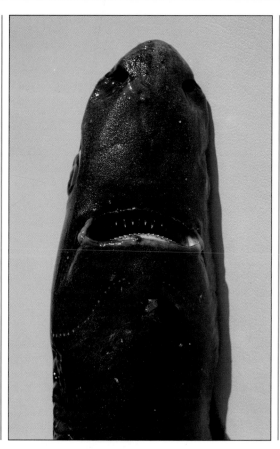

■ *E.SPINAX* – Velvetbelly
E Atlantic and Mediterranean. Grows to 66cm (2ft).
The Velvetbelly is found at depths from as little as
70m down to 2,000m (225 to 6,500ft), but is most
common below 200m (650ft). It is very dark brown
above, with black along the lateral line towards the
tail. The stomach is black In addition to the general
coating of low-level luminous slime, there are light-
producing organs ventrally. It feeds on fishes and
crustaceans. It is ovoviviparous; about six to eight
young some 12cm (4½in) long are born
after a gestation period of six months.

■ *E.UNICOLOR*
NW Pacific. Grows to 50cm (1½ft).

■ *E.VILLOSUS*
Central Pacific. Deep water. Grows to 50cm (1½ft).

■ *E.VIRENS*
Caribbean. Deep water. Grows to 24cm (10in).
Etmopterus virens, also known as the Green or
Lantern shark, is common at depths of around 400–
500m (1,300–1,600ft) in the Gulf of Mexico and the
Caribbean.

It is of particular interest in that it is thought to
hunt in packs. It is only about 25cm (10in) long
when adult, but the stomach contents have revealed
that they feed largely on cephalopods. The cepha-
lopod beaks in the stomach show that as the prey

was substantially larger than this small fish, it is impossible for an individual to hunt and eat the squid. It therefore seems likely that packs may act like terriers to catch their prey.

Euprotomicroides – 1 sp.

■ *E. ZANTEDESCHIA*

S Atlantic. Known from only two specimens, one each side of the S Atlantic. Grows to 42cm (20in).

Euprotomicrus – 1 sp.

■ *E. BISPINATUS*

S Atlantic, Indian and Pacific Oceans.
This species has particularly small dorsal fins. There are many small light-emitting organs, especially on

the ventral surface, which glow with a blue-green light. The light is brightest when the fish is moving but fades when it is still. The fish favours living in central water masses at depths down to 1,500m (4,875ft). At night, however, it is found near, or at, the surface of the sea. Before sunrise it has swum down to the depths to feed on squids or fishes. This remarkable daily vertical migration – more than 1km (½ mile) each dusk and dawn – is a tremendous feat for a fish only 27cm (10in) long and weighing just 70gm (2½oz). Many other central water organisms follow a similar diurnal pattern, although their daily journey may not be so strenuous.

Heteroscymnoides – 1 sp.

■ *H. MARLEYI*

SE Atlantic, SW Indian Ocean. Poorly known. Grows to 28cm (11in).

Isistius – 2 spp.

■ *I. BRASILENSIS* – Cookie-cutter shark

Central regions of Atlantic and Pacific Oceans. Grows to 1.5m (5ft).
The common name of this species alludes to the

circular wounds its jaws create on prey. It is arguably one of the most brilliantly luminous of the squalid sharks. After one was captured at night in 1840, a report on this individual read '... The entire inferior surface of the body and head emitted a greenish phosphorescent gleam, imparting to the creature, by its own light, a truly ghastly and terrific appearance ... the only part of the under surface of the animal which was free from luminosity was the black collar round the throat.'

It was further noted that it lived and luminesced out of water for more than three hours, and that when the fish died, so did its luminosity. Frederick Bennett, surgeon naturalist who made these observations, also recorded that the fish fought fiercely and had torn the net in several places. Many fishermen in succeeding years have referred to the pugnacious and net-destroying capabilities of these small fish.

Isistius has a wide gape producing a circular buccal opening lined with sharp-edged slicing teeth. With these and its strong jaw muscles it can clamp itself on to its prey and take out circular bites. For many years there have been reports of whales and large fishes bearing circular scars on the skin. These scars gave rise to stories of fights with giant squid in the deep seas, because the suckers on the

■ **S.SHERWOODI**
Known only from one corpse washed ashore in New Zealand. Grows to 80cm (2½ft) long.

Scymnodon – 3 spp.

■ **S.OBSCURUS**
Atlantic and Caribbean. Grows to 60cm (2ft).
■ **S.RINGENS**
NE Atlantic. Fish eater. Grows to over 1m (3ft).
■ **S.SQUAMULOSUS** – Velvet dogfish
NW Pacific. Deep water. Grows to 70cm (2½ft).

Somniosus – 3 spp.

■ **S.MICROCEPHALUS** – Greenland or Sleeper shark
N Atlantic and adjacent polar waters. Grows to 6.5m (21ft).

squid arms would also leave circular scars. Now it seems more likely that these 'relics of titanic struggles in the stygian depths' are no more than traces of an *Isistius*'s meal. *Isistius* seems to swallow its teeth shed by natural replacement, rather than just lose them. It is thought that this may be an adaptation to conserve the calcium supply available to the fish because calcium is a scarce commodity in the deep sea.

Isistius has also been known to 'attack' submarine telephone cables and submarines. It is not certain if the fish mistake the submarine for a whale or whether it is the electrical field that attracts it. Certainly it has disabled telephone cables and rendered useless the audio reception of submarines by slicing through the protective insulating covers of cables.

The function of the luminosity is uncertain. It may serve to identify itself to others of its own species; it may act as a camouflage if seen from below; or it may be to attract a large animal near enough to it to bite.

■ **I.PLUTODUS**
NW Pacific and Caribbean. At medium depths. Grows to 40cm (16in)+.

Scymnodalatias – 1 sp.

This giant squalid shark lacks any luminous organs. Usually it lives on or close to the bottom, but in polar regions it is found at the surface and in shallow coastal waters. It is a very passive, sluggish fish. Groups congregate and show some animation around sealing or whaling operations, where they feed enthusiastically. Nonetheless, if caught and taken out of the water, it offers minimal resistance. It is an important part of the Inuit economy because it can be caught through holes in the ice even in midwinter. The skin is used for footwear, the teeth for cutting tools, and the liver oil for many purposes. The flesh is poisonous, however, and unless treated produces symptoms akin to those of a hangover without the alleged pleasure in the production of that condition. The meat has to be dried or boiled in several changes of water before it is palatable to humans or dogs. An important factor in Inuit society, the Greenland shark features in many Eskimo legends.

The sluggishness of this shark is so severe that one observer was puzzled how it was able to catch its food. Nonetheless it does. It is omnivorous, feeding – it is thought – largely on dead mammals and birds as well as fish. One shark was found with a whole reindeer in its stomach. It has not been known to attack humans. Presumably even the most infirm humans move too quickly.

Above ■ Cookie-cutter shark *Isistius brasilensis;* its wide gape and the arrangement of the teeth allow it to excavate a plug of flesh from its prey.

There is an unexplained association between this species and a parasitic copepod. A great majority of Greenland sharks have a parasitic copepod (a crustacean) attached to the cornea of the eye. The copepods *Ommotokoita superba* and *O. elongata* are the two species involved, and they vary from 4mm to 7cm (⅛ to 2¾in) in length. The parasite (and there are rarely more than two per eye – one per eye is the norm) is pale yellow in colour and conspicuous because of the two large egg sacs on each adult. Naturally, the parasites impair the shark's vision; even when the parasites have died, the cornea remains scarred. The only, even unlikely, suggestion to explain this association is that the copepods are luminous and may attract fish close to the shark. Their luminosity has not so far been observed.

The shark is thought to be ovoviviparous. Huge numbers of eggs have been found in large females. Very little is known of its biology.

■ *S. PACIFICUS*

N Pacific and Pacific polar regions. Grows to 7m (23ft). This species is the Pacific counterpart of the Greenland shark.

■ *S. ROSTRATUS*

W Mediterranean and adjacent parts of the Atlantic. Grows to 1.25m (4ft).

This species has some luminous pores along the lateral line. Apart from this and its small size, it is very like the Greenland shark. A similar small form occurs in the north-western Pacific which may be *S. rostratus* or the Pacific equivalent. There is also some doubt whether the Mediterranean population is the same species as the Atlantic population. It is ovoviviparous. Otherwise almost nothing is known about its biology.

Squaliolus – 1 sp.

■ *S. LATICAUDUS*

N and S Atlantic, SW Indian Ocean, W Pacific. Grows to 25cm (10in).

The males of this species mature at about 15cm (6in), and both sexes seem never to exceed 25cm (10in) in total length. It is usually considered to be the smallest shark. Found at depths varying between 200 and 1,200m (650 to 4,000ft), they undergo a substantial daily vertical migration. They are rich dark brown to black in colour and have photophores on the ventral surface. Fishes and squids form the main component of their diet. There are still uncertainties about the details of their reproduction but it seems that they may well be ovoviviparous, producing possibly 10 or 12 young each less than 80mm (½in) long at birth.

Squalus – 9 spp.

■ *S. ACANTHIAS* – Spurdog, Piked or Spiny dogfish

Worldwide in all subtropical, temperate and sub-polar waters at depths from 10 to about 200m (30 to 650ft), even down to 1,000m (3,250ft) in some areas, this dog-fish grows to just over 1.25m (4ft). The Spiny dogfish is probably the world's commonest shark. In Europe it forms over 90% of the commercial dog-fish catch. Its flesh is sold as 'huss' or 'rock salmon' in fish-and-chip shops (other dogfishes, but in smaller amounts, are fried under the same names). A very large specimen may weigh 20kg (44lb) but the great majority weigh only half of that amount. Nevertheless, in 1963 Norway landed over 32,000 metric tons. In 1952 Britain landed 15,000 metric tons, and in 1982 almost 11,000 tons. Many other countries also fish for this species, so its abundance is obvious. However, continued intensive fishing has led to a substantial reduction in the numbers caught. The numbers are still high, but not as astronomically so.

The spurdog is a bottom-living species. Although

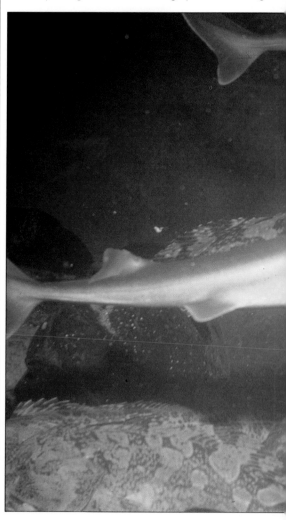

rather sluggish, it does undertake migrations, often in large shoals which feed avidly on their journey. One fish tagged off Newfoundland in July 1942 was caught off Massachusetts in November that year, a linar journey of over 1500km (900 miles). Another fish tagged off Washington State in 1944 was caught off Japan almost eight years later. Seasonal migrations are undertaken so that it stays within the preferred temperature range of 7–15°C (44–58°F).

The spines in front of the dorsal fins that give this species its common name are mildly poisonous and cause an area pricked to tingle, become numb and swell. The end result is a painful, but not fatal, injury.

The fish are grey in colour, paler beneath, and often with white spots which, if present, fade with increasing age. They are ovoviviparous; only one litter of up to ten young is born every two years. The gestation period can itself last for two years, making it among the longest known for vertebrates. The slow rate of reproduction has meant that intensive fishing is likely to rapidly deplete the population which then will not be able to regain its numbers in

time. That there is still a fishery again attests to the initial abundance of this species.

The Spiny dogfish is thought to be a long-lived species; estimates from 30 to 100 years have been given for its lifespan. The male does not become mature until 11 or 12 years old, whereas the female takes 19–20 years to achieve its reproductive potential. This also implies a very slow growth rate because they rarely exceed 1m (3ft) in length.

They feed on practically anything. Apart from the expected fish and crustaceans, they take worms, molluscs of all varieties, jellyfish, algae and any carrion.

■ *S.ASPER*

Caribbean, SW Indian Ocean. Wide depth range. Grows to 1m (3ft).

■ *S.BLAINVILLEI*

Mediterranean, Black Sea, E Atlantic, Caribbean, all southern oceans. Feeds on fishes and squids. Ovoviviparous; one litter of 4–9 pups every other year. Grows to 1.25m (4ft).

■ *S.CUBENSIS*

W Atlantic. Grows to over 1m (3ft).

■ *S.JAPONICUS* – Japanese Spurdog

W Pacific. Deep water. Grows to 90cm (3ft).

■ *S.MEGALOPS*

Pacific and S Indian Oceans. Grows to 75cm (2½ft).

■ *S.MELANURUS*

Central Pacific. Deep water. Grows to 75cm (2½ft).

■ *S.MITSUKURII*

Widespread, except E and S Atlantic. At all depths. Grows to 110cm (3½ft).

■ *S.RANCURELI*

Central Pacific. Poorly known. Grows to 75cm (2½ft).

PRISTIOPHORIFORMES
Saw sharks or Sawfish

Below ■ Sawsharks use their blade-like snouts to disable prey.

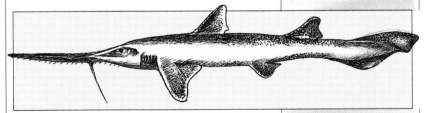

The members of this order are sharks and must not be confused with the superficially very similar Sawfishes of the ray family Pristidae. The pristiophorids, being sharks, do not have the pectoral fins united with the sides of the head; they have free upper eyelids; and the gill openings are on the side of the body, not on the underside as in the pristids. Nonetheless the two groups show a splendid example of convergent evolution.

Saw sharks have a long dorso-ventrally flattened blade for a snout. The sharp triangular teeth along the edges of this blade are modified denticles. They use the saw snout to flail about, damage and catch small fishes on which they feed. It is possible that the saw is used to dislodge food items from the substrate. The jaw teeth are small, single-cusped, and arranged in several rows.

The sharks are ovoviviparous. When the young are born, the teeth of the saws are folded back against the blade to avoid damaging the mother.

Some species may enter fresh water for a short time.

Fossils dating back to the end of the Cretaceous period have been found.

▬▬▬ F A M I L Y 1 ▬▬▬

PRISTIOPHORIDAE 2 genera

Pliotrema – 1 sp.

This genus has six gill slits and no barbels on the underside of the snout.

▪ *P. WARRENI*
SW Indian Ocean. Grows to almost 1.5m (5ft).

Pristiophorus – 4 spp.

This genus has five gill slits and a pair of sensitive barbels or feelers on the underside of the saw.

▪ *P. CIRRATUS* – Common Saw shark
Australia. Often in shallow water. Grows to 1.5m (5ft).

▪ *P. JAPONICUS* – Japanese Sawshark
NW Pacific. Grows to almost 1.5m (5ft).

Below ▪ Pectoral girdle of the Pacific Angel shark *Squatina california*. The width of the large pectoral fins may be as much as half the total body length of Angel sharks.

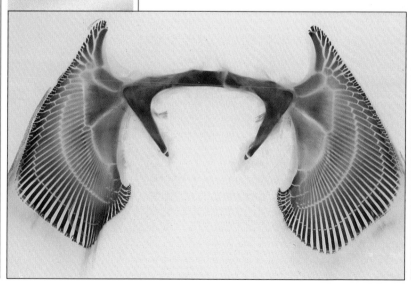

▪ *P. NUDIPINNIS* – Southern Sawshark
Australia. Grows to 1.25m (4ft).

▪ *P. SCHROEDERI* – American Sawshark
NW Atlantic and Caribbean. Bottom-dweller. Grows to 75cm (2½ft).

SQUATINIFORMES
Angel sharks or Monk sharks (fish)

All the members of the one family in this order are dorso-ventrally flattened with greatly expanded pectoral fins that overlap the somewhat expanded pelvic fins. The gill slits are largely on the underside of the body but are in front of the origin of the pectoral fins. The axis of the caudal fin is not turned up as it is in other sharks.

Although they are very skate- or ray-like in general appearance, these fish are considered to be sharks because they have free eyelids, gill openings that extend someway on to the side of the neck, and pectoral fins that are not attached to the sides of the head.

They are all bottom-dwellers, often lying there with their outline disguised by sand or gravel they have nestled into. They can, however, swim actively when seeking prey, which they often do from their camouflaged position of ambush.

Monkfish is an ancient name for these fishes. Guillame Rondelet used it in 1555 in fanciful allusion to one of these fishes he reckoned to look like a sea monk. (He also referred to a sea bishop, and doubtless imagined a clerical hierarchy existing in the seas as well as on land.) 'Angel shark' as a name doubtless stems from a similar source.

These days, the name 'Monkfish' is sometimes also applied to the Angler fish or Goose fish (*Lophius piscatorius*), and the flesh of the tail of this species of bony fish – and indeed the flesh of the Angel shark – has been scooped out with special-shaped cutters and sold as scampi by unscrupulous dealers. The flesh of the Angel shark is tasty and nutritious in its own right: they are caught for human consumption in many parts of the world.

Angel sharks inhabit most of the tropical and temperate waters of the world from the shore to substantial depths depending upon the species. They feed on a wide range of animals that live on or near the bottom. There is a typical shark-like element of casualness in their diet, however. From one stomach a 1kg-/2lb-jar of mustard was retrieved; on another occasion, a slab of wood 45 × 30cm (18 × 12in) was found, studded with nails.

Little is known of their biology. They are ovoviviparous. The European *Squatina squatina* gives birth

Left ■ The Australian Angel shark *Squatina australis* blends in with its preferred shallow water habitat of rough sand extremely well.

to 9–16 pups, depending upon the size of the mother. In this species birth occurs in the summer in northern waters.

Some tagging work and the affixation of transmitters to *Squatina californica* has shown that they swim at depths from about 30 to 100m (100 to 325ft). During one day they may swim up to 9km (6 miles), at a maximum speed of somewhat less than 500m (⅓ mile) per hour. They also ignore water temperature changes when searching for food. They are largely nocturnal, emerging from their shallow cover in the sand or mud at sunset and feeding most actively then and at about midnight. They seem also to have a loosely defined territory of about 150 hectares (375 acres). There is also some evidence that they move into deeper water in winter, when it is likely copulation takes place.

That many of the species have been given common names indicates their, at least former, desirability as human food.

■■■■■■■■ F A M I L Y 1 ■■■■■■■■

SQUATINIDAE 1 genus

Squatina – 13 spp.

■ **S.ACULEATA** – Monkfish
Mediterranean and E Atlantic. Grows to 180cm (6ft).
■ **S.AFRICANA**
SW Indian Ocean. Grows to 1m (3ft).

■ **S.ARGENTINA**
SW Atlantic. Grows to 1.75m (5½ft).
■ **S.AUSTRALIA** – Australian Monkfish
Australia. Grows to 1.5m (5ft). This species was recorded as occurring in Australian waters by William Dampier on 23 August, 1699. This illustration of the fish now known as *Squatina australis* is the first figure of an Australian shark.
■ **S.CALIFORNICA** – Pacific Angel shark
N, NE, E, SE Pacific. Grows to 1.5m (5ft).
■ **S.DUMERIL** – Sand Devil
W Atlantic and Caribbean. Grows to 1.5m (5ft).
■ **S.FORMOSA**
Known only from one specimen caught in deep water off Taiwan.
■ **S.JAPONICA** – Japanese Angel shark
NW Pacific. Grows to 2m (6½ft).
■ **S.NEBULOSA**
NW Pacific. Grows to 1.75m (5½ft).
■ **S.OCULATA** – Smoothback
Mediterranean and SE Atlantic. Grows to over 1.5m (5ft).
■ **S.SQUATINA** – Angel shark or Angel fish
E Atlantic and Mediterranean. Grows to 1.75m (5½ft).
■ **S.TERGOCELLATA**
Australia. Grows to over 50cm (1½ft).
■ **S.TERGOCELLATOIDES**
Known from one specimen caught off Taiwan, 63cm (2ft) long.

NAME INDEX

GENERAL INDEX

STOP PRESS

IMMEDIATELY before publication of this book two new species of shark were discovered and classified, both of the genus *Etmopterus* (see page 117):

■ **E. CARTERI** – Caribbean coast of Colombia. A very small species: all specimens found, from 181–212mm (7–8½in) in length, were sexually mature.

■ **E. PERRYI** – Caribbean coast of Colombia. Probably the world's smallest shark known to date. The males reach sexual maturity at only 160mm (6in) total length. A female specimen 193mm (7½in) long was found to contain three embryos each some 60mm (2½in) with external gills. The species was discovered at a depth of 290m (950ft). It is a very dark grey overall, with some paler lines and markings.